Spiritist Romance

# THE LADY OF THE MANOR

Psychography by
**Vera Lúcia Marinzeck de Carvalho**

By the Spirit
**Antônio Carlos**

**Translation to English:**
## Luis Brayan Ramon Perez
Lima, Peru, May 2024

"A Senhora do Solar"
© Vera Lúcia Marinzeck de Carvalho, 2014
Translated to English from the 1st Portuguese Edition, 2015

Reviewer:
## Sara Molina Oscco

Houston, Texas, USA
E-mail: contact@worldspiritistinstitute.org

## About the Medium

Vera Lúcia Marinzeck de Carvalho (born October 21st at São Sebastião do Paraíso) is a Brazilian spiritist medium.

Since childhood she realized her mediumship, in the form of clairvoyance. A neighbor lent her the first spiritist work she read, "The Spirits' Book", by Allan Kardec. She began to follow the Spiritist Doctrine in 1975.

She received works dictated by the spirits Patrícia, Rosângela, Jussara and Antônio Carlos, with whom she began in psychography, practicing for nine years until the launch of her first work in 1990.

The book "Violetas na Janela", from the spirit of Patrícia, published in 1993, has become a bestseller in Brazil with more than 2 million copies sold having been translated into English and Spanish and adapted to theatre.

This translation of is part of the series of the other three books dictated by his niece Patricia and Antônio Carlos all translated into English and available through the *World Spiritist Institute*.

**Synopsis**

In places of pilgrimage, countless prayers are made, and many of those who make them are receptive and receive graces. How are these requests made? By reading this book, the reader will learn about the dedicated work of those who attend in the name of God, Jesus, Mary, or the saints, as we will see in various places.

Noeli lived a life of deprivation, in which she faced many difficulties. She lived in a house that was deteriorating but that had once been a beautiful residence, a manor house. Why had she been born there? She had glimpses of the past; she remembered the time when she had lived there as a lady, the lady of the manor.

In this book, Antônio Carlos tells us about the possibility of reincarnating in certain places, and there are many reasons for this. These are very interesting stories that, as well as entertaining us, teach us that, through reincarnation, we redeem mistakes, learn, and evolve.

After reading this book, we understand that, in order to respond to a simple request from us, the work of rescuers is usually immense and sometimes mobilizes an entire team.

May God help us to be useful servants so that we can serve and no longer be served.

*I dedicate this book to my granddaughter Isabela, a beloved spirit returning to our lives.*

VERA

São Carlos/SP, 2014

## Contents

- Chapter 1 .................................................................... 8
  - SIMPLE LIFE ........................................................... 8
- Chapter 2 .................................................................. 26
  - LOVE ...................................................................... 26
- Chapter 3 .................................................................. 43
  - LETTERS ................................................................ 43
- Chapter 4 .................................................................. 57
  - VIOLET PARTS ...................................................... 57
- Chapter 5 .................................................................. 75
  - TOGETHER AGAIN ............................................... 75
- Chapter 6 .................................................................. 93
  - BOTH IN THE MANOR HOUSE ............................ 93
- Chapter 7 ................................................................ 106
  - THE MEDIUMS' BOOK ....................................... 106
- Chapter 8 ................................................................ 119
  - ALONE AGAIN ..................................................... 119
- Chapter 9 ................................................................ 137
  - IN THE HOSPITAL ............................................... 137
- Chapter 10 .............................................................. 154
  - CHANGE ............................................................... 154
- Chapter 11 .............................................................. 174
  - THE COLONY ....................................................... 174
- Chapter 12 .............................................................. 189
  - LEARNING TO HELP ........................................... 189

Chapter 13 ............................................................................ 207
   AN INTERESTING CASE ............................................ 207
Chapter 14 ............................................................................ 223
   OTHER TASKS ............................................................. 223
Chapter 15 ............................................................................ 236
   WORK DONE ................................................................ 236

# Chapter 1

## *SIMPLE LIFE*

- Strange! Strange! Celeida shouted at the gate.

- Go on, Noeli, and answer that neighbor, asked Violeta. Noeli, who was in the garden with her mother, went to the gate.

- Good morning, Mrs. Celeida! I'm Noeli[1]! Remember?

- I'm sorry, I keep forgetting your name. I came to exchange. There are almost two kilos of meat here. I want eggs, lettuce, and radish.

Noeli took the package from Celeida's hands and limped away, put it in the kitchen, and returned to the garden, where she and her mother, Violeta, took what Celeida had asked for and went to the gate to deliver the goods, which had been exchanged. The neighbor thanked them and left.

- We'll have meet for lunch today! - exclaimed Violeta.

- Mom, she called me Weird. I have a name!

I don't know why she calls me that.

You shouldn't mind. Don't mind. I like your name.

---

[1] N.A.E: Both Noeli and Noelli are beautiful names. I think that, at the time or in the locality, it was considered a different name, perhaps unusual.

- Mrs. Celeida says it's difficult and that she forgets it, lamented Noeli.

It's not a common name, but it's not difficult.

Why, Mom, did you give me that name? Is it because of the portrait?

- Yes, it was, replied Violeta. When I was pregnant, I paid attention to the portrait on the stairs. My mother said it was a foreign name. I thought the woman in the portrait was so beautiful!

- It's an oil painting, commented Noeli. In fact, she's beautiful, but I don't look like her. Tell me more. I like it when you talk about that time.

While they were working in the garden, Violeta went to her daughter and told her:

His grandfather, Nieto, as everyone called him, was a good man; his name was Antonieto. My father and his grandmother, Maria, came to work in this house when they were two years old. Mom had a son who died of fever. She came to work in the kitchen, and Dad was a coachman. Mom used to say that this house, at the time, was further away from the city, and, over time, the city grew, I don't think by much, and houses were built around here.

Violeta paused, and Noeli thought:

- We're isolated here; the neighbors are far away. The closest is Mr. Danilo; the others are about two hundred meters away. The house is on a corner.

- Come on, Mom, tell us, pleaded Noeli.

Your grandmother Maria took a long time to get pregnant - five years - and I was born, then your uncles Jorge and Zezinho.

You really don't know about them? Your brothers?

- I don't know, replied Violeta. - Jorge left when he was still young; he said he was going to go mining. He wrote a few times and even sent money. One-day Mama was worried and told us that she had seen Jorge, that he had come to say goodbye to her, and that he had died. We sent letters to the last address of the sender of his letters; there were no replies, and he never wrote again. I believe that he has indeed died. Zezinho also left here in search of a job, wrote very little, and, in one of his letters, told us that he had gotten married. When I wrote to him to tell him that Mom had died, he replied laconically, saying that he was moving away, that he was separating from his wife, and that he wasn't going to write anymore. I sent two more letters, and they came back stamped that the person no longer lived there. I never heard from him again.

- Tell me, Mom, about my grandparents, she asked.

They worked here for many years. The manor house had many employees, and over time, everything changed. When Mr. Pietro left, the owner of the place dismissed the other employees, leaving only Dad, Mom, and Sebastian. Mr. Pietro said he was going on a long trip, which would last for years, and left the three of them to look after the house. For two years, he sent his salary to the three of them, then he stopped. Sebastian left, and we were left with my father, my mother, me, and you. In order to survive, my father planted a vegetable garden and enlarged the chicken coop, and we lived off this work. My parents died, and I'm here.

- Mrs. Violeta! - shouted Angela at the gate. I've come to bring bread and pick up some vegetables.

- Come on, Mom, I don't like this Mrs. Angela, complained Noeli. She's always checking me out. Then she's the only one who seems to get the upper hand in the exchanges.

Violeta went to see her.

- I know that people feel sorry for us, thought Violeta, and they help us with trades. Mrs. Celeida brought meat, which is expensive, and eggs and vegetables. I think she wants to help us in this way. But, Mrs. Angela, maybe she's being fair or trying, as my daughter says, to take advantage. Sometimes she brings stale, hard bread.

He answered her.

Noeli went into the house, went to the kitchen, and washed her hands. She would now help her mother make lunch. To save firewood, since the stove was old and made of wood, they cooked lunch and dinner, which was in the afternoon, on a single-burner gas stove.

- We save on everything, thought the girl. The bath water is heated; we only have three light bulbs in this huge house and no appliances. We don't pay for electricity; it was our neighbor, Mr. Danilo, who pulled a wire from his house so we could have this benefit, but we can't abuse it. We have a light bulb in the kitchen, another in the living room to light the stairs, and another in the bathroom that we use.

Noeli decided to go to the bathroom. She climbed the stairs and, on her way down, looked at the paintings on the wall and saw the portrait of the

Lady of the Manor, by Noelli All the paintings, of which there were five, had the names of the portraits at the bottom: Thomas; Noelli; Josefa, Thomas' mother; Eleodora; and Pietro. She had also been registered with the same spelling as the portrait. But even her mother didn't know how to pronounce it, so she was called Noeli.

- Mom says that Grandma used to call her "No-el-li-i.". It's nice. I like my name.

She walked slowly down the stairs; suddenly she saw the beautiful woman, the lady of the manor and, as at other times, she didn't know if it was her who was getting too close or if it was her. She was adjusting her long skirt to step better on the stairs. He smelled her perfume, soft and enveloping, a pleasant scent. It was only for seconds, maybe two. Looking down, she saw her feet were no longer in elegant shoes but in boots. She wore them because one leg was thinner and shorter than the other.

How I wish I were that woman! she sighed.

She went into the kitchen and, together with her mother, prepared lunch.

Angela left satisfied with the change, met Celeida just ahead, and they talked.

- I went to the old manor house to make my change, said Angela.

- I also went to get some vegetables, said Celeida.

- Then I passed by Mr. Danilo's house and talked to him. This neighbor of ours doesn't trade; he buys, so they can have some money. I'm annoyed with myself; I called the girl Weird. She has a different name that I can't remember.

- Do as I do; just call her Violeta, said Angela.

- We help you a lot with these exchanges. In the afternoon, I'll sort out some clothes; my husband bought a blanket, and I'll take it to them tomorrow. Don't worry about forgetting the girl's name. The girl is as different as her name. Ugly girl! She's very thin, has one leg, and walks with a limp. Her eyes are green, more of a dull shade; her right eye is squinted; her chin is large and pointed; and her lips are small and thin, which makes her look very small. Indeed, the girl is strange!

Celeida listened attentively to her neighbor; she had known Angela for a long time. She knew that she only said she was going to take things to the residents of the manor, but she didn't, and she also benefited from the exchanges. And, from the description of the girl, he recognized that it was true, and he felt even worse for having called her by her "nickname".

- I don't think she's pretty either! - exclaimed Celeida. The girl has something I don't know if I can define; maybe that's why she's called Strange!

I don't know why they don't move out of that old house. They're so isolated! - commented Angela.

- Move? Move where? Violeta feels obliged to look after the house.

It's very strange that the only heir to the house, which used to be said to be a manor, has gone away on a trip and hasn't come back yet. Did he die?

- How will we know? - Celeida sighed.

Every time the girl comes to see me, I get the impression that I'm talking to the lady of the manor.

What do you mean?

- Mistress, Angela replied. She seems to be the owner of those ruins.

Celeida preferred to change the subject, and they went home.

In the kitchen, mother and daughter prepared lunch and shared the meat.

We'll keep this piece for tomorrow; this one we'll make into soup for dinner, and this one we'll cook for lunch.

The gap was under the sink. They put water in a basin and put the dish with the meat in it. This prevented ants from getting into the food. It was damp and was always cold, keeping the food from one day to the next.

- Dona Celeida is nice, commented Noeli.

- I even forgot that she called me Strange. Unfortunately, the whole town knows me by that nickname. I loved studying so much that I didn't want to go to school anymore because everyone made fun of me there. I couldn't make any friends. Even Rosiña, Mr. Danilo's daughter, started avoiding me because her classmates laughed at her because of me. I think it would have been better if I had stopped going to school. The most important thing is that I can read and write, I can do math and I know the basics.

My daughter, though Violeta, doesn't get out of the house much. I do the shopping. She doesn't like going out because, unfortunately, people stare at her. I don't think they know that their attitudes offend and hurt my little girl.

They had lunch and went back to work. Their lives were routine; they did the same things all seven days of the week: they tidied the house, kept everything clean, looked after the vegetable garden and the chickens; they had lots of birds that provided them with eggs and meat. In the evenings, they sat in the kitchen, where there was light and where they usually read. Noeli liked to read the books on the shelves in the study, or, as her mother called it, the library. There were lots of books, and she would pick up novels to read. They went to bed early and woke up when the sun came up.

That night, the girl commented:

- Mom, I'm going to take that lidded dish you call a bonbonniere to Mrs. Pérola.

- Is it right to sell household items? Sometimes I think it is, sometimes it isn't. Violeta sighed and continued talking: Mrs. Pérola likes antique pieces and has been buying the ones you bring. This lady must decorate her house in the big city where she lives. Her husband has a farm nearby, and they come here so he can check on the work of his employees. Their house here is also beautiful. Opposite the church square. Do you remember how we met her? Her maid came to buy vegetables and commented that her boss liked antiques. You said you had some, and the maid asked you to take them for Mrs. Pérola to see. I remember you taking out an ashtray.

- And now I always take pieces, and she buys them; with this money, we live better, said Noeli.

And if Mr. Pietro comes back...

- If he comes back, Noeli interrupts. Mom, when he left, I was four years old; today I'm fourteen. So, it's been ten years since he left and eight years since he's heard from us or paid us. Please see these sales as payment.

- Payment for what? - Violeta asked.

- For us being here and taking care of everything.

- That's what worries me, we don't. Nothing is fixed in the house.

- Please, Mama, asked the girl, we're not owners, we're employees. Only the owners make repairs. We need medicine, blankets, warm clothes, and food. You like to drink coffee, and we'll buy the powder. We trade, but we still need a lot of things. I'm going to take advantage of the fact that Mrs. Pérola is in town; she comes here once or twice a month and stays for two or three days to sell something; she buys it and pays for it properly.

- What if Mr. Pietro comes back and asks for these objects? Maybe he'll have us arrested for theft.

- Mom, none of that will happen. First of all, he was detached from what the house had. We can't touch the books he liked or the portraits; the rest he doesn't know he has. Secondly, we can defend ourselves by saying that the lord of the manor didn't pay us. I can't explain it, but I feel that Mr. Pietro is never coming back. Did you like him? As a boss, I mean.

- I saw little of him. He helped Mom in the kitchen, we lived in the back room and my brothers slept in the basement. He didn't go into the kitchen and I hardly ever entered the front of the house.

- Sleeping in the basement! How could that be? - Noeli was indignant.

- In those days, the basement was tidy and clean.

After Jorge and Zezinho left, it became a firewood dump.

- There are so many mysteries in this house! Mr. Pietro's grandmother, who was called Noelli, only had one daughter, Eleodora, and she only had Mr. Pietro. Small family!

- Violeta said, they said that Mrs. Noelli had had a few abortions; they said she cheated on her husband, who was older than her. And when she got pregnant by lovers or didn't know who the father was, she had abortions. She only had one daughter, of whom she was very proud. She married a young man from another town, and he died three years after the wedding, leaving Mrs. Eleodora a widow. But...

- Tell me, Mom, please, Noeli asked.

- My father said that, at the time, Eleodora's husband had fallen in love with a dancer from a big city and wanted to leave with her. Then there was an accident: he fell off his horse, hit his head on a rock, and died. Only Dad said that he was an excellent rider and that the horse was docile. They said that it was Mrs. Noelli who had him killed, that they had seen her giving orders to an employee of Mr. Thomas, the lady's husband, and that this bandit had a reputation for being bad and doing secret services.

- Is this true? Did she have him killed? Noeli asked.

- Dad said yes. They said that Mr. Afonso, the son-in-law, died so there wouldn't be a scandal about his daughter being abandoned and separated. Eleodora became a widow with a little son. She never married again and lived here. Mr. Thomas died, so everyone thought that the lady of the manor was going to marry Mr. João Luiz, her husband's nephew who frequented this house a lot and, they said, was her lover. But he wanted to marry Eleodora. My mother said that there were some fights and João Luiz fell down the stairs and died.

- Jesus Christ! - exclaimed the girl. - I'm glad I didn't see him fall down the stairs.

- Remember what you promised me? Daughter, please don't tell anyone what you see.

- Do you believe me?

- You don't lie, replied Violeta. - I think it's imagination. Talk about your visions only with me.

- Who else do I talk to?

- You talk to the people who trade with us, Mrs. Pérola...

- Noeli defended herself.

- I remind her that this is why she was nicknamed Stranger.

- I hate being called that.

- If you mind, it gets worse, said Violeta.

- Now I know how to control myself. Before, when I had visions of people, I would talk.

- It was difficult when you couldn't control yourself. I even got complaints. Twice from the school. The principal complained that you saw and commented that there was a black man on the back of a cleaning lady and that he treated her like a horse; in fact, this woman complained of back pain. The kids laughed and started calling the employee Black Cargo. Then your teacher complained that you had said that a classmate wouldn't sit still because there was an old woman sitting with him[2]. That's why people were afraid of you. Now let's talk about the sale. I know we need a lot of things, but I don't think it's right to sell household items.

- Mom, the girl pleaded, analyze this with me: before you left, didn't you give your mother's clothes and your grandmother's clothes to the house staff? Didn't you give them bedding and blankets?

- Yes, my parents also received some, said Violeta.

- Mr. Pietro was distracted, not worrying about the house. It was he who was strange, going on a pilgrimage to India. The thing is, he's gone, he hasn't come back yet, and if he does, he won't miss anything because he doesn't know what he's got. I'll sell it and that's it! We've been through enough.

---

[2] N. A. E.: Noeli was a medium. She had the potential to be a mediumship from an early age. And in the case of the employee, it is an exception, the pains are usually physical.

- Okay, you've convinced me, but I don't think it's right! - exclaimed Violet.

- Too bad Mrs. Pérola won't get up early. I'll go at ten o'clock, when she's had breakfast. At that hour I meet a lot of people in the street.

They turned off the kitchen light and went upstairs.

Since Sebastian had left and the back room began to leak, they had felt very ill-accommodated, and when Antonieto died, afraid to sleep in the backyard, the three of them, Maria, Violeta and Noeli, decided to take a room inside the house, the smallest one. The bedrooms were on the upper floor, the house was an annex. Today, the paint is faded and the garden neglected, giving the impression of abandonment. But those who knew it in Thomas and Noelli time knew that it was the most beautiful and luxurious house in the region. Mrs. Eleodora did not take much care of her house, but in her time the garden was carefully tended, with many flowers, and the walls were always painted. Six months after Eleodora's death, her son Pietro, heir to the mansion, left.

Her daughter lay down first; they both slept in the same room, and the bathroom light illuminated the hallway, giving the room enough light to see objects. Noeli had the sensation of lying in a large, luxurious bed, the same one that had been in the master bedroom and was now faded; the headboard was of a velvet that must have been lilac and was now torn and ripped. She felt the linen sheets and the fluffy padding; everything was perfumed. The move was quick, and she soon found herself in a small bed with old sheets and a thin blanket.

I'm going to buy two blankets, one for me and one for Mom. No colder weather for this winter.

She was used to having visions[3]; she didn't even tell her mother.

When the light in the bathroom went out, the room was not dark but was illuminated by a dim light from a street lamp a few meters away. To get this light, they left the window only on the glass side. And so, when the sun came up, it flooded the room with its rays, waking them up.

Tired, they went to sleep.

Early the next morning, Noeli helped her mother in the garden, then changed clothes, took the garment she was going to sell, wrapped it in a towel, and put it in a bag, saying goodbye to her mother and going to Pérola's house. He closed the gate and looked around the house.

Solar! the girl thought. Maybe it really was in the past.

The paint on the once pink house had faded; in many places, it had darkened, and in others, the paint has peeled. Noeli stopped at the wall, one meter and twenty centimeters high, that surrounded the front of the house. The street was dirt, there were no sidewalks, and few people walked on it. Up to Mr. Danilo's house, there was still some movement, but up to the manor house, only people came to exchange goods.

- Noeli! daughter! Violeta shouted, running to the door. I've come to see if you've let your hair down.

- I did, Mama. Goodbye.

Mom was proud of her daughter's hair. It was beautiful, blonde, shiny, straight, and long to her waist. Violeta took care of it; she had learned from her mother to use herbs, and once a week, before washing it, she applied a

---

[3] N. A. E.: At this stage of her life, Noeli called everything she saw and heard from the discarnate, as well as stories of her previous incarnation, a "vision."

mixture of two plants. Then she heated the water and always did it before eating. She would wash them in the basin, where her daughter would sit on a chair and put her head in the place where she hit the clothes. Violet would wash them with other herbs and rinse them with leaves. Her hair would not get tangled, and she would let it dry loose. For two reasons: she washed them before eating, so the water would get hot in the kitchen, and because they took so long to dry.

Mom came in, and Noeli looked around the house again.

- I like it here, but I can't compare it either; it's the only house I know. Mom says we shouldn't compare ourselves with others because comparison is not good: either we think we are superior or we suffer because we feel inferior. And she is right. I am what I am; I live here, and that's it.

Walking slowly, because that way he would limp less, he passed in front of Mr. Danilo's house.

- What a nice man! Polite and helpful.

Danilo's house was large and well-kept. He saw no one and continued walking toward the center of town.

- I don't know why they built a townhouse on such a big lot! Grandma said it was chic then. Mrs. Noelli made the house like in her country.

She came from a country on the European continent. Bedrooms and bathrooms upstairs; living rooms downstairs. Going downstairs and upstairs must have been chic, something luxurious.

She greeted some people in the street and soon arrived at Pérola's house. She rang the doorbell; a maid came to answer it and led her to a room.

- Sit down here, miss. Mrs. Pérola will come to see you.

- It's a beautiful house, thought Noeli. It has so many chandeliers that night must be like day. Nice sofa, expensive objects.

- Good morning! - Pérola entered the room and greeted her. - What have you brought me today?

Noeli responded to the greeting and took the bonbonniere out of her bag. Pérola examined it.

- Do you still have many pieces like this at home? - Pérola asked.

- A few. They are well hidden. I'm selling them because Mr. Pérola authorized it. - Noeli lied.

- He ordered me to sell them and keep the money, as he ordered.

- This piece is beautiful! Do you have any paintings?

- Not many, mostly oil portraits, but we don't have authorization to sell them.

- I will continue to buy your works, said Pérola.

- This one is valuable, isn't it? We need clothes and blankets.

- It's a beautiful piece, but not very valuable. I'll buy it for... - Pérola gave the price.

Noeli thought she would get more. But she accepted. Pérola left the room with the bonbonniere and asked the girl to hold on, she was going to get the money. She came back a few minutes later, paid and gave him a bag.

- You said the money was to buy clothes.

I have some here. Do you want to take it?

- Yes, of course, and I thank you, Noeli replied.

- Maria will also give you another bag. When you have another item to sell, bring it and I'll buy it for you.

They said goodbye.

- What a strange girl! thought Pérola. She just has beautiful hair. I buy these antique pieces, some are valuable. Most of them I resell for a profit. I'm not going to sell this bonbonniere; I like it. I'm going to give the clothes we no longer wear to this little girl.

Maria, the housekeeper, walked Noeli to the door and gave her another bag.

Noeli planned to go to the grocery store to buy coffee for her mother, to a store to buy socks and blankets, and then to order new boots from the shoemaker, Mr. José. But with two bags, one big and heavy, she went home. Curious to know what was in each, she walked as fast as she could. From the door, she called out to her mother.

- I'm in the kitchen, Violeta answered.

- Come and eat, the meal is ready.

- Mom, Mrs. Pérola has given me two bags, one with clothes and the other one I don't know what's in it. Let's see, I'm curious.

- What did she give you? Didn't she buy the bonbonniere?

- She bought it and paid for it. I told her that the items she sold were authorized by Mr. Pietro, that it was our salary and that this money was to buy clothes. She asked me if I could take her and her daughters' clothes, I said yes and she gave them to me.

Curious, they opened the bags.

- Mom, what beautiful clothes! - Noeli exclaimed.

[ 23 ]

- They're still new blouses. They'll fit you and me. This skirt is too short.

They were enthusiastic about the clothes. Most of them would fit.

- The ones we won't wear, said Violet, I'll give them to Maricota or Cida, they have granddaughters who wear these clothes. Open the other bag.

- A loaf of bread, sponge cake, two tins of candy and sandwiches. How delicious! Let's eat!

In the afternoon, they both went shopping. First, they went to the grocery store, then to the tents and bought sheets and two thick blankets.

- There was very little money left, but we bought what we needed! - Violet exclaimed.

- What will we do when all the items are sold? - Violet asked.

- One problem at a time. We still have plenty left. Tomorrow I'll go through each room and take everything I think Mrs. Pérola would like to buy and put it in the library closet.

- There are some toys in the attic, Violet remembered.

- That's the place that leaks the most. Let's take everything out of the attic and put it away. I'll organize all the pieces to sell in the future.

Dinner that night was different. Instead of tea, they had coffee and ate the rest of the sandwiches and cake.

They went to bed happily.

The next day, after eating, Noeli went room by room and took everything she could sell, stuffing it into old sheets. There were jewelry boxes, perfume bottles, metal hangers, soap dishes and lots of silverware. In the parlors, she kept two vases, ashtrays, bowls, cups and plates. She was delighted with the result. In the office or library, there was a large empty space under the bookshelves. Noeli stored the objects there. The next day, she went up to the attic, but didn't find much. Only a trunk with drawings on the wood and toys. With her mother's help, she took the trunk out into the sun and left it in the library.

- This will be the next one I sell, Noeli decided. Because it's made of wood and might have termites in it.

She sorted the toys and took two dolls for herself and the others Violeta decided to give to poor children.

- As a child I loved dolls so much. They are precious.

In the library she had several objects she could sell, but Noeli didn't keep them, she left them where they were: bookends, ashtrays, pencil holders.

These will be the last ones I sell, she determined.

Days passed without news for the inhabitants of the old mansion.

# Chapter 2

## *LOVE*

The life of the two inhabitants of the old mansion was routine, and ten years had already passed. Mother and daughter kept the vegetable garden and chicken coop well cared for. They continued to trade goods and sell them. They had to buy seeds and corn for the poultry, which they also fed with vegetable scraps. Money was scarce, and they were struggling. And for extra expenses, Noeli kept selling household goods to Pérola, who, in addition to buying, gave them clothes and some food. The clothes they didn't wear, those they didn't wear because they were too trendy, Violeta donated to friends who were also poor. The manor house needed more and more repairs, renovations and painting. The roof was leaking badly. Everything was taken out of the attic. Noeli sold the trunks, some of them large, and Pérola sent truckers to pick them up. After many years, someone other than the two of them entered the house.

With much effort, Noeli and Violeta removed some furniture from upstairs and put it downstairs. The room where they slept was still leak-free.

- I'm worried about this house, said Violeta.

- It is becoming a ruin. There is no word about Mr. Pietro.

- Mama, he must really be dead. Do you remember my vision? I went to the library and as I entered, I saw a figure with his back to me near the desk. The figure turned, it was Mr. Pietro and looked at me. I even remember the clothes he was wearing: he was wearing a long tunic with long sleeves, light beige. He smiled and said to me:

- Daughter, none of this interest me anymore, I live elsewhere. Do what you want with all this. God bless you. I was frightened, petrified, unable to move, and the vision evaporated. When I could move and speak, I prayed: Mr. Pietro, please answer me: will you come back?

Where is it? Nothing, no answer. I kept pleading, Mr. Pietro, please answer me: will you come back, can I really sell everything? I went around the room, I looked in the corners, but I didn't see the owner of the mansion and I didn't even feel him.

- You've already told me ten times, Mom complained.

- I'll tell you again so you'll understand: Mr. Pietro has authorized me to sell whatever I want. If it is his and he has given it to me, I can sell it. Mom, why did he call me "daughter"?

- Many people call other people "daughter" or "son", especially the younger ones, in an affectionate way. The owner of this house may have died. He was alone, he has no relatives on his mother's side. As far as I know, Mrs. Noelli came from another country with an aunt, the rest of her family stayed in her home country and lost contact with them. The aunt died when Mrs. Noelli was married. They also say that Mr. Tomas' family was a small one, and after they got married, they quarreled, so he moved away from his relatives. So, Mrs. Eleodora did not live with her relatives. Her husband, Mr. Afonso, had many siblings, but with his death, which was very suspicious, they moved away, and Mr. Pietro had no contact with his father's family, who live far from here. Maybe they don't even know that Mr. Pietro has traveled.

- What a strange family! - Noeli exclaims.

- But I don't have any family either. I only have you. Maybe I have relatives on my father's side. But how do you know? Why don't you like to talk about my father, Mom?

- I've already told you everything, Violet replied.

- You know I don't like to talk about him.

- I know you suffered a lot of prejudice. You were a single mother. You loved him very much, didn't you? I see the souls of the dead; why can't I see my father Fernando's? What was he like? I like to imagine him.

- He was blond, green-eyed, tall and thin.

- Tell me more, please, Noeli asked me.

- We started sneaking out, meeting at the back of the courtyard. He came from another region and told me he had a father, stepmother and twelve siblings. She worked for Mrs. Eleodora. I was wrong to give myself to him, we were thinking of getting married when Ferdinando died. He was delivering cattle and was bitten by a snake. It was two pieces of news together, his death and the fact that I was pregnant. My parents were generous, they didn't scold me, they supported me, and you were born! - Violet sighed.

- Do I look like my father? - Noeli wanted to know.

- Yes, you do.

- Too bad we don't have a picture of him. You can imagine people by their portraits. Mr. Pietro had light brown hair, like his eyes; his mother, Mrs. Eleodora, and Mrs. Noelli were blond. The family of the mansion was light.

- Let's talk about the sale, Mom asked.

- Tomorrow morning I'll take those bookends and the big silver spoons, Noeli decided.

- Isn't that a lot of pieces?

- With the money, I want to buy some netting to re-fence the chicken coop, since ours is old and fraying in several places. Twice some chickens have escaped. They could ruin the garden.

They went to bed. Noeli kept thinking how much she wanted to see her father. She loved him and prayed every night for her father, whom she had never met, and also for her grandparents.

- I will also pray, she said softly, for Mr. Pietro and thank him for giving me permission to sell everything I need.

The next day, around ten o'clock, Noeli got ready, gathered the objects, put them in a big bag, said goodbye to her mother and, walking slowly so as not to hurt her feet, headed for her buyer's house.

- Hello, Miss, greeted Pérola, what have you brought me this time?

- Two pairs of bookends and three silver spoons. This time I brought more because I need to buy new linens for the henhouse. I hope you have money to buy them and that you will offer all you can for these pieces.

-Let's see... Oh, they are beautiful! - exclaimed Pérola. She examined them and quoted the price. This time the seller asked for more, and Pérola agreed. Noeli was happy with the sale and because she had also gotten two bags, one with clothes and one with food. She kept the money, picked up the bags, said thanks and said goodbye.

She decided to take the bags home and go to Mr. Gilson's store first thing the next morning to buy the canvases. He walked slowly.

In front of him, in the square, was a group of boys. Students. One of them, José, was Celeida's son, who had returned home for the Easter vacations and had brought some friends with him. They were studying in a bigger city, where there was a university.

They were sitting on a bench in the square talking.

- I told you there was nothing to do here, said Celeida's son.

- You wanted to come, now don't complain.

- It's all very nice, said one of them.

- Your mother's food is great. It's almost like a field here, the air is clean, and let's rest, we're studying a lot.

- Who is that girl? - asked Antero, one of the boys.

- That weird thing? - asked José.

They all looked discreetly at Noeli, who was crossing the square to get to Pérola's house.

- She's my neighbor, said Celeida's son to his friends.

- This girl and her mother live in an old house that used to be called "ancestral home".

- Is it hers? - one of them asked.

- I don't even know what they are. Mom says that the owner, Mr. Pietro, went on a trip many years ago, left this girl's grandparents to take care of the property and never came back. They say he died and that they both live there, mother and daughter.

- She is very ugly! - commented one of them.

- But she has beautiful hair! - exclaimed Antero.

- Why don't you go out with her?

- I only said she has beautiful hair, repeated Antero.

- You were turned down by Selma, who didn't want to go out with you - said one of the boys.

- You're going through such a run of bad luck that even that girl doesn't want you. What's her name?

- Strange, answered José. - Everybody calls her that. She's older than me, I've known her since I was a kid, although I don't see her much. She has another name. And everyone calls her Stranger because, as you have seen, that is what she is.

- Antero, dear, you can't even go out with her, one of his friends challenged him.

- Of course, I can! - said Antero.

- Shall we bet? - asked one of the other members of the group.

The four boys, who would be in town for three days, burst out laughing. Antero, feeling challenged, accepted the joke. They bet that he, Antero, had to make an appointment with Noeli and spend two hours chatting with her on the garden bench. If this happened, he would win the bet, which was a lottery in which everyone put up a certain amount of money, and if he lost, the group would split it among them all; Antero alone put up four times as much as the rest of the group.

- As far as I know, said Celeida's son, my neighbor will be coming by again soon. I have seen that she has gone to Mrs. Pérola's house and has to go back through the square to go to her house.

- I'm going to talk to her. To do this, I'm going to stand on the other side, on the sidewalk. Get out of here, she can't see you. When I see that she has left that lady's house, I will go to meet her.

The boys went to the other side of the street, they hid, but tried to see what was going on. Antero did what he had planned. When he saw Noeli come out of Pérola's house, which was across the street from the square, he went to meet her. He got distracted and bumped into Noeli. The girl, also distracted, was startled.

- Excuse me, miss. Excuse me. Are you hurt?

- I'm sorry. I didn't hurt myself, Noeli replied.

- Yes, I hurt myself. I sprained my foot! It hurts. Won't you help me?

- How can I?

- Let me lean on you, asked Antero.

- Shall we sit on a bench for a while? I'm sure the pain will go away soon. Please.

Antero held Noeli's right arm tightly and went to the bench. They sat down.

- Thank you, said the young man.

- My name is Antero, and yours?

- Me? My name is Noeli.

- Noeli, a beautiful name. I'm here in town, at a colleague's house.

- I have to go. Does your foot still hurt? - Noeli asked.

- It's better now. But don't leave, not before giving me some information. I'm lost. I'm separated from my friends and I don't know how to get back to the house I'm in. I was trying to get my bearings when I ran into you.

- Who is your friend?

- Jose! - exclaimed Antero.

- Whose son? Do you know?

- His mother's name is Célida, replied Antero.

- They are my neighbors. We live relatively close. I'll explain how to get there.

- Stay here with me a little longer, asked the young man.

- As soon as my foot stops hurting, we'll leave. Can I come with you? If you live near my friend, you can take me.

Antero looked at the girl.

- If I had to describe her, I'd say: tall, slim, blonde and green-eyed. But the nickname is justified: her eyes are narrowed and lifeless green; her lips are very thin; her chin is long; and she's not at all elegant.

Noeli was dressed in a long skirt, she wore it to go out, to hide her thinner leg and the deformity of her foot, the right one was smaller and twisted inward. The blouse was pretty, Pérola had given it to her; she wore boots to walk better.

Antero, wanting to win the bet, was very friendly and chatted incessantly: he talked about the city, asked some questions and paid attention to the answers. After forty minutes sitting, she got up and he kindly took the suitcases and they walked slowly. He talked about poetry and even recited one for her.

- That's where Mrs. Celeida lives, Noeli showed him.

- I live right over there, straight ahead.

- I'll go there and bring her the suitcases. They arrived at the gate of the old manor house.

- Noeli, shall we meet again? - asked Antero.

- Please. On Saturday. I'll wait for you on the bench where we were sitting at 18:30. Please. It's been a pleasure talking to you. It's been years since I've had a good talk.

- I don't know - Noeli was hesitant.

- I'll only take yes; if not, I'm not going.

- Okay, see you Saturday at 20:30.

- I'll be waiting for you. Don't miss me. See you later!

- Antero said goodbye.

He waited for her to open the gate, handed her the bags and, when she closed it, turned and left.

Noeli was happy. For the first time, a young man had paid attention to her, talked about pleasant topics and wanted to see her again. She was giddy with joy.

- He's gorgeous! she thought, Light brown, charming smile, perfect teeth. He's well-dressed, tall, slim and has big hands.

- Noeli, her mother came to help her as soon as she opened the door.

- You took your time, I was worried, what happened? Did Mrs. Pérola keep you waiting?

The girl happily told her about the meeting she had had.

- I don't know if you should go. He's from out of town.

Maybe I won't see him again, worried Violeta.

- Mom must have been traumatized. She went out with Dad, who was from another region. But with me it will be different. Maybe I'll only remember this encounter

- Yes, I will!

Noeli has let herself go, thought Violet. What should I do? I'm afraid she will suffer. I wonder why that young man noticed her. I love my daughter too much, but I recognize that she's not attractive enough to attract boys. What am I thinking? Maybe that boy has realized that Noeli is really a special girl, kind and intelligent. Then it's just a date.

The daughter wanted to change the subject and opened the bags.

- What a beautiful blouse! Look, Mom! I'll wear it on Saturday. Mrs. Pérola didn't want to pay me what I asked for, but this time I negotiated. We need money to buy the chicken coop's tights.

Noeli was different, she was happy and thought a lot about Antero. The next day, Friday, her mother washed her hair better. She chose the clothes she would wear. She kept thinking about the boy.

I must be in love. I'll love him forever, Noeli thought. If he asks me to go out with him, I'll accept. We can correspond by letter. I have a lover! How nice! I'm happy.

On Saturday, the thought of meeting him made her heart pound. She was euphoric. She put off the purchase of the wire mesh until Monday. While tending to the birds, she saw a hole in the mesh, as well as two chickens in the garden. He closed the hole, caught the two runaways, and counted the birds. He noticed that Cocota was not in the coop.

- This Cocota is smart, she is my favorite bird. I'll go look for her.

He looked around the yard and didn't see the hen, so he looked all over the yard. In the soft dirt of a flowerbed, she saw the imprint of her little feet. She followed them. Noeli realized that the bird had broken through the fence, which was very precarious.

The land on which the manor house stood was large and had been fenced with posts and wire. Many pieces had fallen down. At the back of the yard were trees and tall bushes; to the left was a small dirt road with many potholes that descended downhill. A few meters ahead were some small houses, and it was these residents that Violeta and Noeli helped. To get to the center of town, these people used another street; they did not pass that way. To the right of the manor house, where mother and daughter were going to town, after the fence, there was a large open field and then the house of Mr. Danilo. Then there was a small street where there were many houses. This open field overlooked many houses, which they said were neighbors.

Noeli jumped over the fence and saw Cocota near the wall of Celeida's house. Walking slowly so as not to make noise and scare away the scratching bird, she went to catch it. She did so easily, as Cocota was a bird used to her and was docile. She cradled it in her arms and heard voices. It was the boys talking.

- Antero, he thought, is at Mrs. Celeida's house. They're talking, I'm going to listen to them.

- It's the Stranger! - one of the boys heard.

- The girl, though ugly and strange, has a very pretty name: Noeli!

- He recognized Antero's voice.

Noeli felt petrified for a moment. She continued to listen to the young men laughing and talking about her. She looked for a hole in the wall, which was only made of bricks, found a hole and looked through: she saw the young people in the area eating cake and chatting happily. He saw Antero, José and two other young men.

- I'm going to win the bet, said Antero.

- Easy money! I'll sit with her on the bench in the plaza for two hours, chatting. When the time is up, I'll get up, take her home and that's it.

- What if the girl gets carried away and thinks you and she are dating? - Jose asked.

- She won't, Antero replied.

- From what I've talked to her, the girl is no fool. After all, we've all had, have had, or will have an unrequited crush. The important thing is that she wins the bet.

- Let's keep our voices down, José asked.

- If Mom finds out, she'll get mad and stop us from going ahead with the bet.

They began to speak more quietly. To listen, Noeli stuck her ear to the wall and heard some of the words: Noeli, ugly, weird, skinny, bet, money. Antero would have to stay with her for two hours in the square. Then they started talking about studying. The girl looked at them again. She looked at Antero.

I'm looking at him for the last time, she thought.

Cocota lay restlessly in her lap. Tears were streaming down Noeli's face; trying not to make noise, she went back into the house, jumped the fence, left the hen in the coop and went back to check for more holes. She saw her mother in the garden, went into the house and burst into tears. After a few minutes of crying, she washed her face and went to help her mother.

- Where were you?

- Three chickens escaped and I went to look for them, Noeli answered with her head down, not wanting her mother to notice that she had been crying.

When it was time to make lunch, they both went to the kitchen. Then Noeli cried, scaring her mother.

- What had happened to her?

The little girl, sobbing, told her everything she had heard.

Violeta got angry.

- I'm going to tell Celeida. I'm going to insult those boys.

- No, mom! Calm down, please. Let's talk. Those kids are inconsequential, they don't know what they're doing. They play games. They forget that ugly people and strangers have feelings. I'm the one who created expectations and fooled myself. Mom, Mrs. Celeida doesn't know and if she does, the whole town will know and I will be the laughing stock and the joke, even if some people feel sorry for me. I will teach Antero a lesson, I will simply not go to the meeting. I will make him wait, and the lesson will be that he will lose the bet.

- You are right, my daughter. It's better not to go and not to say anything to anyone about this meeting. And if anyone asks, we will smile and say that you had no intention of going and that you didn't even pay attention to the young man. They won't talk, they won't comment on the bet; surely Jose, Celeida's son, will be afraid of his mother. They know they are doing the wrong thing.

Noeli ate very little and her mother prepared a soothing tea for her, which she drank. It was agony for the girl when it was time to change her clothes; she cried hiding in the bathroom. At her mother's insistence, she ate some dinner and went to bed early.

Earlier, the group of young people had gotten ready and gone out to the square. There they separated: Antero sat alone on one bench and his friends on another, from where they could see their colleague. Antero became uneasy, Noeli was late. His friends joined him.

- Antero, you have lost the bet, said José.

- The stranger has not come. The women are late, but not by an hour. We've won!

- I'm going to his house! I have a complex! Not even an ugly woman loves me, lamented Antero.

- Are you really going? - asked one of the boys.

- Yes, I am!

- Then we'll go together and hide. Let's see if she'll accept you. But you lost the bet.

- I lost!

- Antero agreed.

And they left. The boys stayed near the tall bushes, Antero stopped in front of the gate and called out:

- Noeli! Noeli!

Mother and daughter were lying down when they heard him call.

- It's him, Mom! Antero! I'm going to take a look. I'm sure he's so proud that he's indignant that I didn't go! - Noeli exclaimed, getting up.

She looked out of her bedroom window and saw some figures on the floor.

- Her friends had come, they were hiding.

She quickly went downstairs and entered the library, the room at the front of the house, from where she could see the street through the window. She opened the wooden part a little and, through the glass, saw Antero in front of the gate. It was dark, but she could see him; he was still, then she picked up some pebbles, threw them at the front door and shouted louder:

- Noeli! Noeli! Come here, please, why didn't you go to meet him? Have you forgotten? Noeli!

The girl looked at him. Violeta got up and went after her daughter.

-Do you want me to pour water on it? - asked her mother.

- No, mom, we won't do anything. I'm sure she'll be gone soon.

They heard a whistle; his friends were calling him. Antero left. Noeli closed the window and went up to her room with her mother. They didn't talk. It took him a long time to fall asleep. She could hear her mother snoring.

- I will only remember what I thought was good about this event: the bump, our conversation, him walking me home, the poetry.... And forget the joke, about the bet. If I were a normal girl, his attitude wouldn't have changed a bit, but I'm not; I'm strange, the ugly girl. Perhaps he and his friends will never know the wrong they have done me.

The next day, she got up at the usual time and saw herself in the mirror dejected and sad. Violet was sad too.

Why, my God, is my daughter like this? I think she's pretty because I love her, but if you look at her, her physique is ugly. Does she look like her father? I don't know what to do.

The best thing to do is to be patient and wait, time heals all wounds. I won't tell anyone what happened.

- Mom, please go see the clients today. I will stay in the garden.

Violet agreed, but that Easter Sunday few people came to trade or buy vegetables. Taking advantage of the fact that her mother was talking to a woman, Noeli took the same path as the day before and approached the wall. She peered through the hole. She saw the boys getting ready to leave and playing with Antero. He imagined that his friends were teasing him for losing the bet. They left the area and went inside. Noeli figured they were going to catch the ten o'clock bus. He returned home. Her mother made no comment about her daughter's absence.

They went to lunch. As Noeli sat back in her chair, she had another vision. She saw herself in a long skirt of luxurious fabric, sitting and crossing her legs.

- Oh no! It's not a vision today! - she exclaimed. Violet made no comment; they ate in silence.

Early the next morning, the girl went to Mr. Gilson's store and bought the canvas and the iron pipes to fix it. She also bought what her mother liked: coffee, candies and sweets. She spent almost all the money she received from Pérola.

- Mom deserves it! She's the only one who loves me, he thought.

Mr. Gilson promised to deliver the goods in the afternoon. Noeli worked hard the next few days, in the vegetable garden and changing the chicken wire, but when she worked hard, her feet and ankles hurt a lot. Her mother made her herbal compresses and gave her soothing herbal teas.

My foot hurts, Noeli thought, but the physical pain is still less than the pain in my soul. With the tiredness, my body wants to rest and I will sleep. I will strive to do what I have decided and I will keep this love in a drawer of my soul. There it will be. The Stranger loved, had a love. It will only be a memory. Life goes on. It is my life that I have to love.

She finished the chicken coop and decided to enlarge the vegetable garden. Work helped her, as it helps everyone. When we have a lot of time, our problems tend to increase. No one else heard about the boys' mischief. Her routine returned to normal.

Although she tried hard not to remember Antero, Noeli thought about him a lot and cried because she missed him and because she loved him and was not reciprocated. She decided never to deceive herself again and promised herself that she would never be interested in anyone else. She came to the conclusion that it was better to have loved someone and to have suffered than never to have loved at all. She felt better when she could pray for the boys and Antero, wishing them happiness.

# Chapter 3

## *LETTERS*

The years passed, and few things changed. Their lives were always the same, they performed the same tasks every day. They got up early; they ate bread or sponge cake; when they were full, they drank coffee or tea; they went to the garden; they took care of the chickens; they served the customers; they made the food; they ate; they cleaned the house; and they went to the garden again. In the evening, after dinner, they would read a little and go to bed. There was not much news, the shopkeepers would tell of village happenings, gossip, and some would complain about life. Violeta was the one who went out to do some shopping, and Noeli only rarely went to Pérola's house to sell something.

I only have two pieces that might interest Mrs. Pérola, Noeli thought. There are also books and paintings. She has already said she is not interested in books. My buyer hasn't been in town much. She told me she's sick and her children don't want to come. Last year, she only came twice.

- Mom, said Noeli, tomorrow is my thirty-fifth birthday. Time passes slowly, but at the same time fast, I feel old.

-I do feel old, said Violeta, smiling.

- Daughter, sometimes I think that, if everything happens as it should, I'll die before you.

- Don't say that, Mama, please. Don't talk about dying. What am I going to do without you?

- You'll live until it's time for you to go to the afterlife. Promise me, child? Please! If I die, you can go on with your little life here.

- Mom, you've been talking about death a lot lately. Why is that?

- It would be nice if we died together! - Violet exclaimed.

- But that will certainly be difficult. You know a lot

You see so many spirits! If I could, child, I would never separate from you. Do you know why? Because, we love each other very much. Then, if you see spirits, you'll see me. I really wish you'd die before me. I really do! Maybe I'll live better on my own. Because I know that if you die, you'll go to heaven.

- We don't even go to church, Noeli comments.

- But we pray, and I feel God in me, with us. We didn't sin. We haven't done anything wrong. I don't think God the Father considers it a sin not to go to Mass, which is an external act. Mom, are we going to move our bedroom downstairs today? To the private room? The rainy season is coming soon, and there are many leaks upstairs. We'll take one piece of furniture at a time and carefully move downstairs.

- I don't like to tinker around the house, Violet replied, but we have no choice. Since there's no bathroom downstairs, we'll have to keep going upstairs.

- But at least we won't have to sleep with leaks. It must have been very chic to have a room in the house all to yourself, an intimate room, like Mrs. Noelia and then Mrs. Eleodora had.

- 'I think it was for receiving friends,' said Violet, someone to chat with in private. There were some precious objects there that we sold. Let's clear out first. We'll move the sofa, which is very old, to the corner of the room, and we'll also have to remove the small tables. Our two beds have to fit in the small room.

- That long piece of furniture is too heavy, it has to stay there, and we'll store our clothes in it. Are we going to do it now? - Noeli asked.

The mother and daughter entered the small room, the door of which opened into the living room. At the entrance to the house, there was a hallway which, at that moment, had nothing in it, because the two pieces of furniture that were there, a coat rack and a small table made entirely of marquetry, had been sold. From the hallway there was a large living room, which was also almost empty; Noeli had already sold the furniture that was better and nicer. In the living room there were many doors: the office/library, never knew what that room was really called; another door was the intimate sitting room, which had been used to receive private visitors; an archway separated the living room from the dining room; and then there was the kitchen. In the living room was also the staircase leading to the upper floor, where the bedrooms and two bathrooms were located.

They took the sofa, which was moldy, like many pieces of wood in the house, and left it in a corner of the room. They took out two chairs so old that they were no longer usable.

- Mom, shall we use them for firewood?

- That's the best we can do. This chair can't even hold you up; you're so thin. It was in this chair that Mrs. Eleodora liked to sit. Once I came to serve tea, and she was standing in front of the window embroidering.

- Was she pretty? She doesn't show much in the picture, Noeli wanted to know.

- Maybe she wasn't as pretty as her mother or as elegant. She was always alone. When her mother died, she and her son were left; then he went to study in another city, and Mrs. Eleodora was very lonely.

Although she worked here, I saw her very little. Sometimes I saw her when she went to mass on Sundays, and on those occasions she always wore black. She did not have many friends.

- What did she die of? - her daughter asked.

- She was sick, she vomited a lot and when she died, she was very thin. Do you remember her?

- I remember very few things from that time. I remember once I saw Mr. Pietro looking at me. I don't know how I remember; I was four years old.

They were silent for a moment and then Noeli asked, changing the subject:

- Mom, do you miss my father?

- What do you mean?

- My father?

- It's been so many years... - Violeta answered. I don't forget Antero, thought her daughter. I don't feel anger or resentment towards him. I prefer to think that he paid attention to me and was kind. I'm sure he doesn't even remember me. It's okay, I remember him. It's a love I hide in the back of my mind. Even mom doesn't know about it. It's my secret, only mine.

- Let's clear this piece of furniture so we can put the clothes inside. What's the name of this piece? - Violeta asked.

Noeli had a vision. The woman, or herself, as she felt, very well dressed, her hair neatly combed in a bun, was bending down to pick up something from the piece of furniture. Her long earrings came up to her face and she heard, I wonder where that box is

- Is it here, on the counter? The vision disappeared.

- It's the counter! - Noeli exclaimed.

- What did you say? - Mom didn't understand.

- This piece is called a counter. Pass me the cloth, I'll clean it.

Noeli always had visions, two or four a month. Most were with his wife, Noelli, and when they happened, he felt like he was her. He couldn't understand his visions. When he saw spirits, it was easier, but rarer: he saw his grandmother and others, some accompanying shoppers.

The daughter picked up the wet cloth. Mom sighed. Noeli stopped and looked at her; she knew that when her mother sighed, it was because she was remembering the past and was going to talk about something she remembered. Since he liked to listen to her, he waited looking at her.

- I think everyone who has lived in this mansion has felt lonely.

- Could it be that even the first residents felt lonely?

- Mrs. Noelli, said Violeta, came from another country and had only one aunt, who must have found her a husband as soon as possible. Mr. Tomas was old and ugly.

- Indeed, thought Noeli, that's what happened, her aunt got her a marriage, either she got married or she went to work as a nanny.

- Mrs. Noelli married her husband without wanting to! - Noeli exclaimed.

- 'Sometimes, I think you know a lot about the lives of former residents,' said Violet.

- Don't forget my visions, Mama. I have only come to the conclusion that the marriage of Mr. Thomas and Mrs. Noelli was not for love, at least on her part. Poor thing!

- Mr. Thomas built this house just as his young wife wanted, Violet continued.

- He furnished it, and they came to live here. He, the eldest, didn't like traveling or parties. He distanced himself from his family and was only friends with a nephew who visited them a lot and who everyone said was the owner of the manor house. Mr. Thomas had farms with cattle and various crops, they lived in luxury, but I think they were isolated.

- He was very jealous of his young wife, Noeli interrupted. - I can feel it. She had few friends.

- They had only one daughter, Doña Eleodora, and they raised her like a princess. Mr. Thomas loved his daughter very much. In this house, there was always a garden with many herbs, and it was some of these herbs that Mrs. Noelli used to make abortifacient infusions.

- Did it always work? - Noeli asked.

- I don't know. Maybe, if it didn't work, she used other methods. I didn't want to have any more children. When I found out I was pregnant, I was almost four months along. I know because you were born at five months. Mrs. Eleodora advised your grandmother Maria to make the infusions and give them to me. We talked (your grandfather, my mother and I) and decided not to kill the child I was carrying in my womb. Your grandmother Maria used the term "kill"; for her, abortion was murder.

- And for you, right? - Noeli asked.

- If it's a living being, when you abort it, you kill it. The important thing is that I had you that you were the most precious gift I ever received, given to me by God. Let's go back to the subject of loneliness. I think Mr. Thomas must have been lonely, fighting with his family, having a wife who did not understand him. Mrs. Noelli, a young woman, who lived here, far from the city, must not have liked it and surely felt very lonely, because her daughter, at the age of ten, was going to boarding school, and it was in the city where she was studying that she met Mr. Afonso. It didn't help that her parents were against it, and Mrs. Eleodora married him.

- He soon got fed up with this monotonous and perhaps lonely life, took a lover and was going to run away with her, when Mrs. Noelli had him killed. I don't know why she doesn't strike me as a murderer.

- My father used to tell me that he and other servants of the house saw her giving orders to one of the servants and that day Mr. Afonso died. And then there was more loneliness. D. Thomas became ill, suffered a lot and died. His nephew, D. João Luiz, began to come home more often. Everyone thought that the lady of the house would marry him. Then the accident happened, he fell down the stairs and died. Both mother and daughter were widowed here with the child. Mrs. Noelli died, and Mrs. Eleodora did not manage well what she had inherited. On the farms, crops became scarce, livestock dwindled, and they say that so that Mr. Pietro could study, she sold land. She died alone in her room. As she was slow to get up, Didiña, a maid, went to call her and found her dead. She died during the night.

- Then - Noeli interrupted again

- Mr. Pietro came, who was also strange, because he was in the capital and nobody knew what he was doing. He sold all the land, kept only this house, organized and went to India, didn't he?

- I always thought Mr. Pietro was different. Sometimes he would scream in his sleep, saying that someone was chasing him.

- A soul from another world? - Noeli wanted to know.

- I don't know, I don't know. I think he had visions of the dead.

- Like me?

- I think it was worse, because he saw evil spirits. Mom overheard him talking to his mother once, where he complained about seeing his grandfather and father fighting. She said she suffered with those visions and didn't want to stay in the manor house. I remember when Mr. Pietro said goodbye; he was dressed for a trip, took the three servants by the hand and said, Take care of everything. Goodbye.

- I wonder what he was doing in India? - asked his daughter.

- My father told us that he had heard him say he was going to "get together". Let's get back to work. Clean that piece of furniture right away, Violeta asked.

Noeli started to clean it. It was empty. Previously there had been some drink bottles that had been thrown away, as well as bowls, glasses and cups that had been sold.

- It's a big piece of furniture, all our clothes will fit in here, which are few, said her daughter.

- We'll be fine here, this room is smaller, but it doesn't leak.

They both wore a lot of long, baggy pants, sometimes Noeli wore long skirts. They preferred discreet colors, but since they won almost all the clothes, they wore what they had.

- It sounds hollow in here, listen to the noise, Noeli said.

- It does indeed sound hollow.

Noeli knocked on the wood and looked at the back of the counter to the right.

- Mom! There's a false bottom here.

She pulled hard on the wood and it came loose. She picked up what was inside.

- Look, Mom, two sheets of paper, they look like letters, a bracelet and a pair of earrings.

Noeli got up and went to the window, where there was lighter

- These jewels look like silver. They are precious pieces. I'm going to sell them. Mrs. Pérola's maid said she would be in town this weekend.

- Could we sell them? They must have belonged to Mrs. Noelli or Mrs. Eleodora, said Violeta.

Her daughter looked at them, the earrings were long, handcrafted pieces, like the bracelet.

- They did not belong to Mrs. Noelli Surely; she would not wear such simple jewelry. I feel they were not hers. I don't think I've ever seen these before. I'll give them a good wash, I'm sure they'll look better.

- We don't need anything important right now. Money depreciates quickly. Isn't it better to keep them?

- Mom, you know Mrs. Pérola doesn't come to town much. I have to take advantage when she comes. I'll sell them, take the money and buy what I can keep: clothes and food that won't spoil... sugar, salt, oil... I'll read the letters... There are two and both are for Mrs. Eleodora.... The first one is from her husband, when they were engaged, Mr. Afonso wrote swearing eternal love. False! Because years after they were married, he cheated on her and left with the other woman. It was he who gave her this gift, this jewel. I am sure that Mrs. Eleodora kept it after the betrayal and forgot about it. I will read the other letter... Mom! It's from Mr. João Luiz. He wrote that he loved her and wanted to marry her. He wrote that he knew that there was a strong obstacle. He confessed that he had been seduced by a woman and that he had even though he loved her, that it had been a wrong implication, which he regretted very much. He begged Eleodora to come to her senses and give him a chance to show her how much he loved her and that he thought about her all the time.

- Everyone knew, Violeta commented, even the servants, that the lady of the house had lovers and that João Luiz was her favorite. I think that when she was widowed, she planned to marry her husband's nephew.

- And then he wanted to marry her daughter, heiress to Mr. Thomas' fortune.

- Maybe Mr. João Luiz really loved Mrs. Eleodora, her mother commented.

- He did not love her. - Noeli was blunt in her statement. - What he loved was money. He never worked; he was an adventurer. He saw in the naivety of a widow abandoned by her husband a way to continue his good life without working. He deserved to die!

- Noeli! Daughter!

The girl kept silent and looked at her mother, who had been startled.

- It was nothing, Mom! It came into my head and I spoke Don't be frightened. It's none of my business. Let's burn these letters. We're not moving tomorrow. First, we'll look through all the furniture to see if we can find anything else hidden so we can sell it.

They cleaned the little room thoroughly and made it ready for the move. Then they went up to the attic.

- There's nothing left here. I think if I were to hide anything here, it would be in the walls, commented Violet.

They went room by room. Violet went to the orchard, and Noeli to the room Mrs. Noelli occupied. She looked in detail. The closet was empty, as was everything else. She reached in, tapped, pulled out the drawers and found a gap. She reached in and pulled out what was inside: letters and a brooch, a beautiful jewel adorned with red and green stones.

- This place must be worth a lot! - he exclaimed.

He read the papers, two letters and a note. He recognized the handwriting of one of the letters and the unsigned note as being from Mr. João Luiz. The note read only: "Don't forget Uncle Thomas. Come to my room tonight or I will miss you very much."

- I remember it! - Noeli exclaimed quietly.

- The lady would give her husband herbal teas that made him sleep, and she would leave the room and spend the night in the guest room.

She would read the letters. The one from João Luiz spoke of love and asked for money.

- Sure, he would do it! - Noeli lamented.

The other letter was from a certain Feliciano and, from what she read, he loved the owner of the mansion very much.

- He must have been another lover. But she must have loved Mr. João Luiz very much. I will burn these papers and keep the brooch.

She only showed the jewel to her mother.

- There must not be anything else upstairs, otherwise she would have found it. I'll keep the brooch and sell only the bracelet and the earring. Next week, I'll look for it downstairs. I've only kept one glass vase and if I find anything else, it's a guarantee for the future. this painting! I can't wait to open it.

There were two paintings in the living room.

- This is the smaller one. - Violeta commented. - It's the painting of the manor house, only a little different. I think they described the place to the painter, who didn't come here.

They took the painting off the wall and the mark remained.

- How painting influences a house! The painting is faded and ugly! - the daughter lamented.

She picked up the painting and examined it.

- I'm going to sell these paintings, Noeli thought with determination. When I've finished everything, I have to sell; I'll take them to Mrs. Pérola. They may not be worth much, but they'll buy food.

Running her hands over the back of the canvas, she noticed that they had pasted another piece of paper on the bottom and that there was a bulge in the center. Her mother protested, not wanting her daughter to open it, but tore the paper off. Noeli carefully unfolded it and read what it said.

- My God! - Noeli exclaimed.

- What is it, my daughter?

- They were Mr. Thomas's papers. There are accounts in this one. Here is a receipt for what the previous owner paid for the painting. On this sheet is something written, I think by Mr. Thomas. Listen to this: From what you told me; João Luiz is my son. The male child I didn't have with my wife. I don't know why I got involved with my sister-in-law. I hope no one knows.

- I don't think we should look any further. How many mysteries this house contains! - exclaimed Violeta.

- I'm curious and I'm going to look some more. Now I'm going to look behind all the pictures. Help me, Mom, to take them off the wall.

It was easy with the other two in the living room.

They didn't find anything. The ones on the wall by the stairs were harder. Violet grabbed a chair, her daughter climbed up and ran her hand over the pictures. They were dirty, but they found nothing else.

- I'm going to burn these papers, Noeli decided. - They are secrets! That's why they weren't happy in this mansion.

So much trouble! Mr. Thomas married when he was older, had an affair with his sister-in-law when he was young and thought that Mr. João Luiz was his son, so he took him, the only relative, into his house. His wife was his stepson's mistress. When Mr. Thomas died, Mr. João Luiz wanted to marry his cousin, who was actually his sister. If he had not died, he would certainly have married her.

She put the pictures on the wall.

There are so many secrets to this old house! thought Noeli.

The two of them returned to the garden and commented on what they had discovered.

- Mom, did you know what we found?

- Me? I didn't know. I've never heard any comments about it. You seem to know more than I do. Did a vision tell you?

- No. I've never seen Mr. Thomas or his nephew. I always see Grandma Maria, some of the old employees, I've seen Mrs. Eleodora crying around the house. I asked her why she was crying, she didn't answer and disappeared. I've also seen Mr. Pietro that time he authorized me to sell everything I wanted, at least I think that's what he meant. What I see most is me as Mrs. Noelli. Don't scold me, Mom, you don't understand. I must confess that even I don't understand. But that's how I feel. The lady of the manor is so close to me that I think it's her and that it's me, I see glimpses of the former owner coming down the stairs in her elegant shoes, holding her dress, walking upright, her head held high, her hair always well combed, wearing jewelry, lipstick on her lips. I also see her in front of the mirror, getting ready and sometimes sitting at the table waiting for her meal. She didn't eat much so as not to put on weight. Now I don't eat much because I have nothing to eat. What a mystery! They say I'm strange, but it's life that's strange.

# Chapter 4

## *VIOLET PARTS*

In the garden, they soon heard Nalva shouting for Violeta, who went to answer her.

- I want lettuce and two dozen eggs. I didn't bring anything to exchange, I'll pay. Where's your daughter?

- In the garden.

Nalva wanted to say "your daughter". She abbreviated it and, like the other customers, in order not to call Noeli a stranger, she began to ask Violeta about her as "her daughter" or "her dater!", until it became Sofia, which was a common name in that town. And so, Noeli became, in addition to Weird, Sofia.

- Better Sofia than Weird," commented Noeli. - Sofia means "wisdom". Mrs. Nalva's daughter, who studies philosophy, told me that Sofia means "wisdom". I'd like to be wise, to have a lot of knowledge.

- You shouldn't mind, Sofia is also a beautiful name, advised her mother.

The next day, Noeli went to the office and looked everywhere, finding nothing hidden.

She got very tired because she even moved her books and took the opportunity to clean everything. In the evening, she went into her room and looked at the dolls: there were two that had belonged to Eleodora, found in a chest in the attic. Her mother wanted to give them to poor children, but her daughter wouldn't let her:

They're for decoration, she argued. Violeta washed the dolls' clothes, put them in order, and they stayed in her room: during the day, on top of Noeli's bed; at night, she put them on a chair. She liked them. When her mother wasn't there, her daughter would pick them up as if they were a baby.

I so wish I'd had a son! Someone to call 'mom'. I even thought about adopting. But who would give me a child? We're poor, Mom is already old, and with this sick leg, I've been walking more and more difficult, I've had a lot of pain in my foot, ankle and back. Sometimes it's hard to get out of bed. I'm going to buy two new mattresses with the money I'll get from Mrs. Pérola. I hope she buys the jewelry.

She put the dolls back.

The next day, at ten o'clock, she went to Pérola's house with her bracelet and earrings. As she passed the square, she looked at the bench and felt nostalgic.

Maybe I should have gone to the meeting even though I knew it was a bet, she thought. I'd have more things to remember. I can't explain how much I loved and still love Antero. Maybe I deluded myself because I was so lonely. I don't know about him, he must have graduated, got married and doesn't even remember this town anymore. It's okay, I remember him.

He continued on his way. He waited a while for Pérola in the living room, and the maid served him coffee and cake.

When the owner of the house came to see her, she had eaten all the cake. After the greetings, Pearl examined the bracelet and earrings.

- They're old, but silver isn't worth much.

- I thought I'd get more money. I wanted to buy two mattresses, the one Mom and I sleep on is bad.

- So, I'll pay you more than they're worth, said the buyer.

Pérola glanced covertly at Noeli and thought:

- She looks older than she is. This woman's life isn't easy. I've already made money on the pieces I've bought from her. I'll pay more.

- Do you have any more things that might interest me? - Pearl wanted to know. - I'm asking because I haven't been here much, maybe I won't come back this year. My husband is ill and my children don't want to come to this city anymore.

- I only have a few things: a brooch, a crystal vase and the paintings.

- If you want to bring them, I'll buy them.

- I don't know. It's just that money, with this inflation, soon loses its value, Noeli explained.

- You can buy things and keep them. Like mattresses, warm clothes, non-perishable food, have boots made for you.

The two looked down at Noeli's boots. They were old and worn out. It was an old shoemaker who used to make her boots. The one with the crooked foot was smaller and had a higher heel. One foot was completely different from the other.

Maybe Mrs. Pérola is right, thought Violeta's daughter. I'll sell the vase and the brooch and do what she told me. If she doesn't buy it anymore, who will I sell it to?

- Can I bring it to you in the afternoon?

- I'll pay for these jewels now, and we'll agree on the price of the other pieces in the afternoon. Take these bags.

- Thank you!

Carrying the three bags, Noeli left. As she passed the square, the priest called out to her.

- Nolma! Noelza! Ma'am, please, can I talk to you?

Noeli smiled, even Father Ambrózio mistook her name.

He knew him by sight.

- How are you, Father Ambrózio?

- I'm fine. Come into the church with me, the priest asked.

She accompanied him. They entered and sat down on a bench. Noeli looked around the church. She had always found it beautiful: the colorful stained-glass windows, the wooden benches, the altar with the images of the saints... She had only been there a few times, and most of those times had been when she was a girl and still studying. She hadn't been to church for a long time. The priest waited for her to look around, then asked:

- Isn't God's house beautiful?

- House of God?

- Yes, the church is the house of God, replied the priest.

- Does God only live here?

- In all the churches.

- And the rest? The universe? In people's homes? - Noeli asked.

- Well, maybe he visits those places.

- Hmm...

- You don't believe me? - asked the priest.

- I think God is everywhere.

- He is as well, I think God is everywhere, agreed Father Ambrózio and changed the subject.

- I called you here because I don't see you or your mother in church. Are you both Catholics?

- Yes, we are. I was baptized in this church; my grandparents were my godparents. Mom and I pray a lot. On Sunday, we say the rosary. We don't go to mass because Sunday morning we're busy in the garden.

Two women entered the church, looked at the two of them and didn't hide their surprise. The priest greeted them and they knelt down next to them, perhaps to listen to the conversation.

- Father Ambrózio, perhaps now you understand why I don't come to church. The faithful wouldn't pay attention to the Mass.

The priest understood, smiled and spoke:

- They would get used to it.

- That wouldn't have to happen, after all, I'm not green. I don't know why I attract so much attention, Noeli sighed.

The priest smiled again and spoke quietly so that the two women wouldn't hear.

- That's fine. But if you need me, come and find me. If I can, I'll help you.

Noeli felt like giving alms to the church, but thought:

- God, I'm currently poor. I'm sorry if I don't give anything to your house, I'd rather give it to Mrs. Cida, who even goes hungry. Sometimes Mom and I go hungry too.

- Thank you, Father Ambrózio, and lowering his voice, he said, if you need it, I'll ask for it. I'll be right there. Thank you!

She got up, picked up her bags and left the church. She didn't say goodbye; she didn't want to kiss the priest's hand. She went home. Her mother was waiting for her for lunch. While she was eating, Noeli told her everything that had happened.

- I don't think it's a sin not to go to Mass, said Violeta.

- Of course not, Mom. It's not wrong not to attend external events. Angela came into the church and pretended not to know me; she only greeted the priest. She goes to church a lot and is such a gossip! I bet she'll come here soon to find out what the priest said to me. If that happens, pretend you don't know.

Violeta agreed. They opened the bags and put away the things that Pérola had given them: some clothes; old but good bath towels; and some ready-made food, bread, cakes, cookies and sweets.

A few minutes later, they heard Angela calling them.

- Violet! Sofia!

Her mother went to answer her.

- I just want a dozen eggs. And Sofia? Hasn't she arrived yet? I saw her in church talking to Father Ambrózio. Did she tell you what they said?

- No, I didn't even know my daughter had been to church. What's so great about going to church? Isn't it public? If you saw her there, it's because she was also in church.

- Oh yes! I go to church a lot. I'm just curious, I don't see you there.

Noeli decided to talk to her neighbor. Knowing her, she knew that Angela wouldn't leave until she knew what had happened and then told everyone.

- Mrs. Angela, said Violeta's daughter, I went to church because Father Ambrózio, when he saw me passing through the square, called me in and only invited me and my mother to go to mass. I told him that at mass time we were working in the vegetable garden. That was all. Have you paid for the eggs? Come on, Mom, get in, we've got a lot to do.

- What were you doing in the square at that time? - Angela asked.

- What do you do in the square? Walk! Don't you pass by? Good afternoon, Angela!

Noeli replied, took her mother by the hand and went inside.

Angela then had to leave.

- Mom, I'm going back to Mrs. Pérola's at 3 o'clock. I'm taking the vase and the brooch.

- That's all we have left.

- Mrs. Pérola says she's going to come to town less and less. I'm going to sell and buy some good mattresses for us, pillows, new netting for the chicken coop and, so that the money doesn't fall in value, I'm going to spend the rest on corn for the chickens, seeds and food for us. If we need money later on, I'll sell the paintings and the furniture in the office/library, they're the only ones that are any good.

- Before, said Violeta, I didn't think it was right for you to sell these objects, but now I think it is, because if the only heir hasn't come back yet, it's because he must have died, and if you had a vision of him, and Mr. Pietro gave you the objects, then they are yours. If you didn't sell them, we would be in more need and these objects would deteriorate.

Noeli stayed to help her mother until it was time to go to Pérola's house. She wrapped the vase in a towel and put the brooch in her pocket.

Pérola was amazed by the vase, but she really liked the brooch and paid a lot for them. Noeli was delighted; she had never seen so much money before.

- Have another boot made, advised Pérola.

- I think you should make three. The shoemaker, Mr. José, is old; if he dies, maybe you won't find another one who can make them properly and who doesn't charge too much.

Noeli thanked him and went home. On Saturday night and Sunday, mother and daughter made plans on how to spend the money.

On Monday, Noeli went to the cobbler's early in the morning, ordered three pairs of boots and paid for them.

I'll have boots for many years, she thought happily.

Then she went to a furniture store and bought two new mattresses and pillows. Then he went to a clothes store and bought some clothes. Then she went to Mr. Gilson's store and bought some canvas for the chicken coop, sacks of corn and food. She came home hungry; her mother had already eaten lunch.

- Mom, soon Mr. Gilson will send the things I bought, I'm going to keep them in that corner in the living room. It's the best place, it doesn't rain and it's not damp.

The mattresses were delivered, two boys left them in the living room, and they exchanged the old ones for the new ones.

- I'm going to give the ones we used to use to Cida, said Violeta.

- Mom, first ask her if she wants them.

- If you sleep on the floor, on straw, you'll like these.

- When we think, concluded her daughter, that we're at our worst, there are people worse off than us. Do as you wish.

Soon after, they received what they had bought from Mr. Gilson.

- Mom, there's only this money left.

- I'm going to buy some sheets and we'll save the rest.

The two of them couldn't stand working in the garden any longer. Violeta felt tired and Noeli complained of pains in her feet and back. They decided to invest more in the chickens.

- Let's pray more tonight, decided Violeta.

- This bed smells so good. It's the first time I've slept on a new mattress and pillow that didn't come from someone else.

They prayed.

Two months passed. Violeta was talking a lot about deaths. She told her daughter about the deaths of her parents, the men of the manor and some of her acquaintances.

- At Mrs. Noeli's funeral, there were many people and flowers. Mr. Pietro was a boy and cried a lot. Mrs. Eleodora dressed in black, looked serious, but didn't cry. I know that everyone reacts in different ways.

When I die...

- Please, Mom - Noeli interrupted

- Don't say that!

- Daughter, death is for everyone. Maybe you'll die before I do; if that happens, I'll pray for you and I don't want to cry too much.

- I know, so as not to wet my wings and prevent you from flying up to heaven.

- My mother, your grandmother Maria, was the one who said this, she said that crying doesn't let the deceased rest.

- Mom, is it really true that Mrs. Eleodora laughed when she came back from her mother's funeral?

- There are people who laugh out of nervousness. But perhaps she felt relieved. I think that the lady of the manor, because she was beautiful, overshadowed her daughter, and I think that Mrs. Eleodora didn't receive a mother's love. She must have been hurt by her mother for not letting her marry Mr. João Luiz. But, back to the subject, of course, if you die before I do, I'll miss you very much. And if I die first, you will too. However, I really want you to do your best. You'll eat well, pray and send me kisses.

At every opportunity, Violeta talked about the separation that would occur if she died. She worried a lot about her daughter being alone and asked God to take her first, promising that if this happened, she wouldn't cry or regret it.

One night, at dawn, Violeta felt ill and woke up her daughter, who got up frightened and lit another candle.

- What's wrong with you? What are you feeling?

- Chest pain and shortness of breath, replied her mother, panting.

- I'm going to ask Mr. Danilo for help.

- No! Stay with me. I want to talk to you. It's about your father. - Violeta held her daughter's hand and spoke slowly.

- Ferdinand is not your father. Back then, we only looked at each other, we didn't date. I... I was raped.

Noeli stared at her mother in amazement. Violeta paused and continued speaking:

- I used to go there a lot, as a child and young man, in that corner to the left, at the back of the yard. My father had made a swing in the mango tree, and my brothers and I would go there to play and swing. I was there alone, it was late in the afternoon when I was assaulted, the man had his face covered. It was horrible! It wasn't Ferdinand because he was traveling and died that day, he was far from here. I told Mom because I came home dirty, with my clothes torn and bruised. We couldn't hide it from Dad. Unfortunately, in those days it was worse, women were blamed for suffering violence. They would say that I dressed inappropriately and that I shouldn't have been out in the backyard alone. By that time, my brothers had already left. Even though my mother begged me not to, my father went around the yard with a machete and found no one suspicious. We decided not to tell anyone about it. Four months later, I found out I was pregnant. So, Dad told Mrs. Eleodora, who only said: "I don't want people talking about rape, not in my house. It's best to say that the child is Ferdinand's, who is dead. If you agree, you can stay here, and I'll even help you". In fact, she bought clothes for me and the baby.

- Rape! How you must have suffered!

- It was indeed a difficult time! But you were a gift from God. I love you very much! Forgive me for not telling you. Your grandparents and I decided that we would tell you when you were grown up. They died, and I didn't have the courage.

Noeli saw her grandmother Maria standing by the bed. She signaled sharply for the vision to move away.

- Leave my mother alone! - Violeta asked.

- Do you see her? - Noeli asked.

- I can feel her. Daughter, don't forget what you promised me...

Violeta kept quiet; she was panting heavily. Noeli didn't know what to do: stay there or go for help, go to Mr. Danilo's house and beg for help.

- Like my mother, your grandmother Maria came to stay with me at this time, and I, like your mother, will also be able to stay with you - Violeta spoke with more difficulty.

- Promise to keep living! Promise me!

- Yes, Mom, I promise!

- I love you. Don't forget! Am I going? I'm ready. I'm going!

Violeta closed her eyes; her breathing was very difficult. Noeli was as if petrified, she held her mother's hands and watched as she calmed down and her breathing stopped. She saw a vision of her grandmother and two other figures running their hands over her mother's body, then her grandmother Maria picked her up and her little mother turned into two[4]. Maria cradled her daughter in her lap like a baby, smiled at her granddaughter and they left. The room, which until then had been bright with the departure of the visions, became dark. Noeli remained still, not knowing what to do.

---

[4] N. A. E.: Noeli witnessed her mother's death. As soon as her physical body stopped working, Violeta deserved to receive help from good spirits and to be taken to a rescue center. Good people usually die this way, receiving a reaction from their good deeds.

- My God, help me! - pleaded Violeta's daughter.

- What should I do now?

- Pack everything up and then ask Mr. Danilo for help - she heard.

- Vision, please help me!

Calmly, because she was getting help, Noeli picked up an outfit, the one her mother liked best, put it on, tidied it up, combed her mother's hair, then got changed. She saw that the sun was rising over the horizon. She left the house, walking slowly, and went to ask for help at Danilo's house.

She clapped her hands and shouted for her neighbor, who opened the door a few moments later.

- Noelma! Sofia! Has something happened?

- Mr. Danilo, Mom's dead!

- What's wrong? Are you sure? Wait a minute, I'm going to change and check this out.

Indeed, a few minutes later, Danilo and Olga, his wife, went with her to the manor house and accompanied her to her room. As soon as Danilo saw Violeta, he realized that his neighbor was dead. Olga hugged Noeli, struggled and managed to speak:

- I'm sorry!

- I'll take care of everything for you, said Danilo.

- Stay here, I'll bring the coffin. Do you know where to bury her?

- My grandparents were buried in the local cemetery, in a small grave. I wanted to bury her with them.

Noeli cried. The couple stood still, looking at her. She wiped away her tears.

- Let's go now, we'll be back soon, said Danilo's wife.

Olga felt afraid, she didn't want to stay there.

- Miss, said Danilo, who preferred to call her that, affectionately, so as not to get her name wrong, while I'm making the arrangements, do whatever you have to do. It might take a couple of hours or more. The best thing is to take the body to the little room in the cemetery to be veiled. I'll be back as soon as I can.

- You're an angel! - Noeli exclaimed.

The couple left and she decided to do what Danilo had suggested. She took care of the chickens, fed them plenty of corn and collected the eggs. Then she lit the fire, made coffee, had it and ate a piece of bread. He tidied himself up.

He put the money he had saved in his pocket. Maybe I'll need it, he thought.

He waited in his room and prayed to God that his mother would be all right. She heard a call and quickly opened the door. It was Olga with the doctor.

- Sofia, I've come with the doctor, he has to certify her death so we can bury her.

The three of them entered the room. The doctor asked a few questions, examined Violeta's body and confirmed that she had indeed died. He signed a piece of paper, gave it to Olga and said goodbye. Noeli accompanied them to the door. A few minutes later, a car pulled up in front of the house, and Noeli answered it; there were two men with Danilo, carrying the coffin. At that moment, the resident of the manor house felt desperate; they were going to take her mother away.

- No! No! - the vision told her. - A body without a soul is like old clothes that you take off. Be strong! They're doing their job. Every job deserves respect!

Calmly, she accompanied the three men to the bedroom, and the two of them carefully placed Violeta's body in the coffin.

- Can we go now? - one of the men asked Danilo.

- Yes. Come on, miss.

They placed the coffin behind the vehicle and closed the door. The four of them settled into the car seats and set off. A few minutes later, they arrived at the cemetery. In front, there were two rooms with small benches[5]. They placed the coffin in the middle of the room. Georgia, a lady who grew and sold flowers, entered the room.

- Mrs. Georgia, please bring me these flowers - Noeli took the money out of her pocket and handed it to the florist.

- I'll bring the most beautiful ones! - Georgia exclaimed.

-Mr. Danilo, said Noeli, I don't have any more money, the one I gave to Mrs. Georgia was all I had. Please pay for the funeral for me; I'll pay you back as soon as I can.

- You don't have to pay me. You really don't have to! I could do it and I did. Take it as a gift.

- Thank you, is too little to say thank you. I may never be able to repay you, but God can. Thank you so much!

---

[5] N. A. E.: At that time and in that location, they weren't called wake rooms. In this cemetery, there were two reception halls which, in special cases, served as a wake. Danilo, this charitable man, decided that it would be better for his neighbor to have her mother buried there. Later, these rooms were enlarged and, as in many places, lifeless bodies were laid to rest in them. It's good to have proper places for these purposes, to help the deceased with prayers and heartfelt prayers, and for the relatives gathered there to be consoled with affection and friendship. When we go to a wake, we should act as we would like to be acted upon at the wake of a loved one. Certainly, at ours, we would like to be respected, nurtured and wished well.

She sat down next to the coffin. Soon Georgia returned to the room with lots of flowers, they decorated the coffin and put the rest in two vases. Noeli seemed oblivious, some people came over, greeted her and prayed; she just thanked them and stared at her mother's lifeless body the whole time. Father Ambrózio went to give the blessing and consoled the daughter.

- Miss! Sofia! Your mother has gone to heaven!

When the priest left, Danilo pulled her by the hand.

- Go to the bathroom. I'll wait for you here!

Noeli obeyed, went to the bathroom, washed her face and felt better. Danilo took her to another room.

- Eat this and drink this coffee! - Danilo ordered. Even though he didn't want to, he obeyed. She felt better.

- Miss, said Danilo, we're going to bury your mother later, in two hours, at fourteen. That's because a storm is forecast. Are you all, right?

- Yes, sir, thank you.

- Don't say thank you, Danilo interrupted. - Neighbors are there to help.

Noeli went back to the coffin. It was time to say goodbye, and she kissed her mother's cold face. They closed the coffin, and it hurt so much that she felt as if her chest would break. Few people attended the wake and even fewer accompanied the coffin to the grave.

She watched as they closed the tomb. She couldn't believe that her mother's body, which she loved so much, would remain there.

How painful separation is! she thought.

- All right, miss, let's get out of here before the rain, said Danilo.

She returned home in the generous neighbor's car, which dropped her off at the gate. Noeli went into the house, closed the door and cried loudly for minutes.

- How sad my life will be! I'm all alone! - she lamented.

Then, crying, she went to look after the chickens. Soon it began to thunder and lightning flashed across the sky.

- It seems that the weather, the sky, is crying with me! As you predicted, it rained a lot.

- I don't need to water the garden; I've already taken care of the chickens. I'll stay here in the kitchen. I have to get used to being alone. If Mom were here, we'd have dinner.

The rain is fine. The storm has passed.

- Miss! Sofia!

Noeli heard Danilo calling her. She ran to open the door.

- Mr. Danilo, come in, don't stand in the rain.

- I'm protected by this cloak. I've brought you some soup. Olga made dinner earlier. Please eat!

- I don't know how...

- You're welcome. Take care, miss! Make an effort! Try! Good night!

Noeli was alone again. The soup was appetizing, and she ate it. She saved the rest for the next day. She went to her room.

- Tomorrow I'll take everything of Mama's that isn't good for me and I'll take it to Mrs. Cida. She was wearing a torn dress at the wake.

She picked up a doll and wrapped it around her like a baby.

- She'll be my little girl! The daughter I didn't have! Feeling tired, she lay down, prayed and slept. Life had to go on.

# Chapter 5

## *TOGETHER AGAIN*

It was very difficult for the resident of the manor to do everything on her own. She concluded that she wouldn't be able to cope. That morning, she had already stopped cleaning the chicken coop five times to attend to the customers.

- I've brought you lunch ready, meat and rice, said Nalva.

- Thank you so much! It smells great!

That day, it was a week since Violeta had changed her plans. Her neighbors and customers were doing this, bringing ready-made food. Noeli was grateful for both the food and the affection.

This will pass! she thought, sighing. Soon everything will be back to normal. All of them, neighbors and customers, are good people, but they have their problems, difficulties in their daily lives. Unfortunately, these treats will become scarce until they run out. They feel sorry for me, they knew how close Mom and I were. How much I miss her! It was a sacrifice to wash my hair. I left everything tidy, the herbs close by and turned my head. I can't manage on my own!

She thought, while eating her lunch, that Nalva's food was very tasty.

I definitely won't be able to do all the work. So, I'll plan what I'm going to do. I'll only clean the parts of the house I use: the bedroom, kitchen and bathroom.

Once a week, I'll clean the living room, the office, the stairs and sweep the front of the house. I'm going to stop with the vegetable patch, I won't plant any more, I'll sell the vegetables in the bed until they're finished. The income will fall, and I might go hungry. There's no other way. How hard my life is without Mom!

He put what he had planned into practice. He didn't plant anymore; the seeds remained in storage and would, in the future, be food for the chickens. She watered what was left of the vegetables, served the customers, cleaned the house and got so tired that she didn't feel like doing anything else. She left the two beds in her room and gave away only her mother's clothes, which didn't fit her.

I certainly won't be able to buy clothes, blankets, anything. I have to save on everything to feed myself. Now I'm going to wash clothes. If it was hard with Mom and me working, it's gotten worse, much worse.

And just as she had predicted, the neighbors stopped bringing ready-made food. With vegetables becoming scarce, they looked for eggs and chickens.

- What a lonely life, I talk so little. I have to buy some food and I have to go at a time when customers don't usually come, from twelve to fourteen. I have little money, so I'll buy the essentials.

Three months had passed since Noeli became an orphan. And, as she had promised her mother, she avoided crying and mourning and tried to look after herself. In the evenings it was worse: she would lock up the house and sit in the kitchen reading, but she couldn't concentrate. She had been using a magnifying glass to read for a long time, and her eyes couldn't see as well as they used to. She was always tired and her ankle hurt a lot. She went to her room early, prayed and couldn't stop crying. She consoled herself with her dolls. That night, she picked them up and hugged them. She had a vision. She was right there in her room, but she saw the Lady of the Manor in the old intimate room. I don't want any more children! the vision complained softly. No! No more boring Eleodora, who's as ugly as her father. I want to stay beautiful for them, for him, to have a statuesque body. Children are a nuisance! They cry and want their mother. A horror! No more children! I'm going to abort this one. I don't want to! Noeli was so frightened that she dropped a doll on the floor. She quickly picked it up again.

So that's it, she thought. Mrs. Noelli didn't like her daughter and didn't want any more children. And I, who want children so much, don't have any. What does the lady of the manor have to do with me? I'm living here now, in the ruined house, in need and alone. What is this fate? Why all this?

I don't understand, but I feel, when I have these visions, that I am the former owner of this house. How can that be? I'd better try to sleep, this vision was very sad, depressing. I would never have an abortion, not even if I had been raped like my mother was. Who would my father be? Would he have known that I was born because of his evil act? The best thing is to forgive him. I don't need a father!

Five months had passed since her mother had left, and she was counting the days. She didn't go to the cemetery anymore, because she was sure her mother wouldn't be there. Her life was too monotonous. As she had little vegetables, the customers were coming less.

- It's a good thing Mr. Danilo didn't want me to pay him. I wouldn't have been able to.

That night, he went to bed early, his exhausted body crying out for rest. He lit the oil-fueled candle and placed it, as he always did, on the counter, because the old room didn't get any light, it was very dark. He used to lock the door.

She woke up to a noise. She got up in distress and became alert. She heard it again. There was a knock on the front door. She put on a coat, opened the bedroom door, took the candle and slowly went into the living room and approached the window that overlooked the area in front of the door. He saw a figure lying near the door. He heard moans. For a moment, he didn't know what to do. He took a deep breath and asked:

- Who is it? Who's there?

- Help me! I'm hurt!

She heard a male voice.

- What am I supposed to do? Is there no vision here to help me? Nothing! I can't feel a thing! Is it true? It must be.

He looked again and seemed to see blood.

Do unto others as you would have them do unto you. I'm going to open it, and may God protect me, she thought determinedly.

Noeli opened the door, holding the candlestick with the burning candle. She came across a fallen man. He was still young, maybe twenty-five, wearing simple clothes and a coat that looked new and good.

- Help me, lady of the manor!

She passed the candle over him to give him a better view. The man was lying on his back and there was blood on his clothes. Startled, she saw a knife sticking out of his abdomen.

- Don't be scared! Please! I'm hurt! - pleaded the man.

- What should I do? - asked the resident of the house, very frightened.

- I'm all alone. I'm going to die. Stay with me. Let me see you. You look different.

- Who are you? Why are you here?

- I think I came here to die. I don't know. In this life I haven't killed anyone and I've been murdered. It's the law! I used to live in another city and came with some acquaintances to this region to look for work. My companions decided to steal. We got into a fight. I ran away, deserted the group. I was on horseback. By instinct, I came to this town. I knew I had to come here. The gang came after me, found me near here, wounded me and left me lying there, thinking I was dead. I got up, walked with difficulty and came for help.

- The young man struggled to speak. give me some water! Please!

Noeli went quickly to the kitchen, filled a mug with water, brought it back, bent down and poured water into the injured man's mouth.

- I'm going to get help. My neighbor will surely take you to the doctor.

- No! Please! - the young man looked at her.

- There's nothing you can do. I've lost a lot of blood. If I take the knife out, the bleeding will become intense. I'm going to die, I know. You look different, Lady of the Manor. Very different. Where are your nice clothes?

- I can't let him die like this! I... - exclaimed Noeli.

- For God's sake! Stay with me. I don't want to die alone. Can you pray? Pray for me.

- What's your name? - she asked.

- Thomas! No! My name is Antônio!

- Do you feel pain?

- It hurt more before; the young man replied with difficulty.

Noeli took a towel and put it under the young man's head.

- I see luxury, a lot of luxury and wealth. What was the point? I had to see what a ruin it had become. Noelli.

- How do you know my name?

- I don't know my name. Pray, asked the wounded man.

Noeli placed the candlestick on the floor next to him. She was kneeling, in pain, she got up and prayed aloud. Hail Mary, then Our Father and, when she recited the part about asking for forgiveness, she commented:

- Good Father, forgive us out of charity. Forgive us!

Do you, Antônio, forgive?

- Yes, I do, and I want God's forgiveness! Madam, I have a wad of money in my coat pocket. Take it for yourself. Please!

She bent down, searched through her coat pockets, found it and picked it up.

- What else do you want me to do? - asked the resident of the house.

- Ask God to help me. I feel like I'm dying. Pray again.

As she had already seen her mother die, Noeli concluded that this man was also dying. She asked her grandmother Maria for help.

- Grandma - she prayed - help this soul! Our Father... She saw her grandmother approach the wounded man and speak:

- He's leaving. I recognize him, he's the old Mr. Thomas. It will take longer to turn him off. Pray, my granddaughter, until he stops breathing. Do it out loud. Then go back to your room. Tomorrow morning, ask Mr. Danilo for help and tell him that you found him in the morning.

Noeli prayed aloud. Antônio couldn't speak anymore, he was panting. Suddenly, he calmed down and stopped breathing.

- He's dead! - exclaimed Noeli. - He's gone from this world to the next! Go in peace! May Grandma Maria help you!

Following her grandmother's recommendation, she took the candle, entered the house, locked the door and went to her room.

Won't his companions come after him? The money?

He counted out the money in the packet, it wasn't much and concluded that his old cronies wouldn't risk themselves for so little. It'll buy food. He gave it to me, so it's mine. Very strange! Am I not dreaming? No, I'm awake. This young man said he came by instinct. He called me by name. He seemed to know what it was like here in the past. He first said his name was Thomas.

He went to bed, but couldn't sleep, thinking that there was a corpse in the house. He prayed a lot and calculated that it must have been two o'clock when he woke up to the man knocking on the door. She ended up falling asleep and woke up startled when the sun rose, got up, changed her clothes, got ready and went to the front door. The man seemed to be asleep, the knife was still buried in him and his face was calm. She looked around in the bright sunshine and saw that the young man was ugly, light brown, with curly hair, but his features were inharmonious.

- He's young! she sighed regretfully.

She bent down and searched her pockets to try and find something else, but only found a bloodstained handkerchief. The boy had no papers. She took off the towel she had put over his head and went quickly to Mr. Danilo's house. The neighbor opened the door, startled.

- Mr. Danilo, there's a dead man in the house. It was like this: I got up, opened the door and saw a man lying there. He's not breathing and there's a knife in his stomach.

- Wait a minute, I'll change and go there, said Danilo.

A few minutes later, he and his wife accompanied her.

- Here it is! - Noeli showed him the fallen man.

- Oh my God! How did he end up here? - asked Olga.

- I don't know, replied the manor resident.

- What can I do?

- Calm down! I'll get the police! - said Danilo.

The neighboring couple left, Noeli closed the door and went to make some tea. Soon Danilo returned with the deputy and two policemen.

- What's your name? - asked the deputy.

- Noeli.

- Tell us what happened, asked the deputy.

Will he think I killed him?

Grandma, what should I do?

She saw her grandmother standing next to her and, calmer, told her what had been recommended.

- I got up, opened the door and was startled. I saw the man lying there. I put my hand in front of his nose and realized he wasn't breathing. I asked Mr. Danilo for help.

That morning was busy. The neighbors, seeing the police car in front of the manor house, went to see what had happened. The deputy took the body away, and Noeli repeated what the police had said many times.

She washed the area to get the blood off. Thankfully, no one doubted what she had said.

Am I lying or omitting a fact? she thought, annoyed.

I didn't used to lie.

But if I tell, I'll have to pay back the money he gave me. With the money, at least I won't go hungry for six months.

In the afternoon, Danilo shouted at the gate for his neighbor.

Noeli promptly went to answer him. He was accompanied by about eight women, neighbors and customers.

Nalva explained:

- Mr. Danilo went to the police station and came to tell you what the police had found out. As he said he was only going to talk to you, we accompanied him to listen.

- Miss, Danilo explained, the police found out, because they followed the blood trails that the dead man left behind, that he was wounded at the northern entrance to the city, which is not far from here, if you go through the outskirts. They tracked down his parents, the boy's name was Antônio and he's from the neighboring town. His mother said that her son was keeping company with an untrustworthy group. The delegate passed the investigation on to his colleague from the boy's home town. That's all!

- Thank you, Mr. Danilo, for everything, said Noeli.

- This boy, commented Nalva, must have been wounded, he came walking and, when he saw the big house, he easily entered the area, where he fell and died. I'll pray for him!

Danilo left, and the women stayed for almost an hour talking about it.

- Antônio, concluded the resident of the old manor house, spoke the truth. I'm glad they saw the traces of blood. For a moment, I was afraid of being accused of murdering him. It was a busy day, and Noeli liked it, it was a break from routine. The next day, she went to buy food with the

money she had earned from Antônio.

Two months had passed since the day Antônio had died in the manor house, and everything was back to normal again. After lunch, Noeli went to the bathroom and, as she went downstairs, she saw a sight that impressed her. She saw Noelli very nervous, arguing with someone in her room.

She felt slighted, annoyed that she hadn't managed to get João Luiz to do what she wanted. He left the room nervously; he didn't like being contradicted either. He was already in the stairwell when she came after him and caught up with him. The lady from the manor house said softly: You won't leave me! No! No! And no! You won't marry her! Never! He replied in a tone so low that surely only she could hear: It's over! Understand! You've finished what you should never have started! I want to have children! Marry her! Her vision flickered and she tried to catch him by the coat, but he dodged, stepped wrong and rolled down the stairs with a clatter. Noelli was startled and ran into the bedroom. He went into his room, unbuttoned his vest and let his hair down. A maid knocked on the door, she opened it and asked: What are those screams? What happened? An accident, run! Come and help, replied the maid. The lady of the manor, panting, buttoning her vest, went downstairs. She saw a worried Eleodora and a servant examining João Luiz's body. He's not breathing! said the servant. Noelli bent down and tried to see if he was breathing. - I can't hear anything. Run, get the doctor! It's better not to touch him. What happened? - I think he fell down the stairs, Eleodora replied, or he was pushed. - She didn't answer, she got up, started giving orders and thought: It wasn't my fault! I only went to pick him up! It was better this way! Traitor! I couldn't let him marry my daughter! Mama, she heard Eleodora say, are you satisfied now? She didn't want me to marry him. I hate her for this. I'll never forgive her. Jealous!

The vision disappeared. Noeli sat down on the step. She cried softly. It had been the greatest vision she had ever seen, and it had been very clear.

Why do I feel like I'm the former Lady of the Manor?! Why?

My God!

When she calmed down, she got up, went to the kitchen and made herself a calming cup of tea.

Does she have a reason for having this vision? As I understand it, when Mr. Thomas died, Mrs. Noelli thought she was going to marry Mr. João Luiz, but he wanted to marry her daughter. They quarreled, she followed him and, on the stairs, they quarreled once again, he fell and died. It's best to forget that vision. If Mom were here, I'd tell her. I can't tell anyone, so it's best to forget.

She sipped her tea and heard a noise outside the house. Thinking it was a customer, she got up and opened the door. He didn't see anyone at the gate. He heard another noise, this time coming from the vegetable garden.

- Who's there?

Noeli asked, and when they didn't answer, she felt afraid. Alert, she looked around. She saw dirt being removed from the radish bed. Without making a sound, she approached the bed. She saw a small figure running to her left.

It's a crafty child. He's come to steal radishes. I'll surprise her!

Walking slowly, he went to the mango tree and saw the child leaning against the trunk, eating the radish and looking at the house.

- Ah, naughty boy! - Noeli exclaimed loudly.

The poor "child" was so frightened that he jumped. She grabbed him by the shirt. Then she looked at it. It wasn't a child, but a dwarf. She had seen a dwarf once before in the city and also in pictures in magazines. She tried not to show astonishment or admiration.

-Robbing my garden? Why? - she asked.

- I'm hungry, replied the intruder.

- You must be, to eat a radish without peeling it. Why are you here?

- I was passing by, I saw the garden, I couldn't see anyone.

I grabbed a radish.

- Where do you live?

- I don't have a house.

- Do you have a family? - Noeli wanted to know.

- No, I'm on my own.

She had made lunch and dinner, as usual.

She decided to give him her food.

- Come with me! I'll feed you. His eyes lit up and he followed her.

- Sit here!

He sat down in the chair, she made a plate of his dinner and gave it to him, who started to eat, he was really hungry.

- Excuse me, he asked, I'm hungry, and the food is very tasty.

Quickly, he ate it all. She only had a little left and put it in for him.

I'll have bread and tea for dinner, he thought. Now, slowly, he ate it all.

- Thank you very much!

- Now you can go.

- Where to? - he asked.

- What do you mean "where"? To your house.

- Didn't I say I don't have a home or a family? Can't you find me a job? Your garden needs tending.

- Do you understand horticulture? - Noeli asked.

- No, but I can learn.

- What's your name?

- Sneeze! - he replied.

- Name?

- Pingo, Espirro.

- You don't have a name? A real name? That's a nickname.

- I don't have one. I'd better tell you everything, he decided. - I don't know if I have or had a name. I was born this way, small, I'm a dwarf. We lived on a farm far from the city. Then I was Pingo. My mother died and my father soon remarried. I think my stepmother sold me to the circus owner. She must have told my father that I ran away. I was eight years old. As far as I know, my father didn't go after me. At the circus, I was given the name Espirro. I learned to work, to be funny, I was a clown.

- Didn't she like it? - Noeli, interested, wanted to know.

- As with everything in life, there are pros and cons. When the pros outweigh the cons, everything is fine; when it's the cons, it gets difficult. Being a clown, making people laugh, is a natural thing, people are born that way; forcing it complicates things, because it doesn't come naturally. I had to.

- Didn't you please the audience?

- Yes, people laughed, he replied.

- But I didn't like it. The worst thing wasn't the performances, it was that I was mistreated. Look! - He lifted up his shirt.

- Look at my back! They're always scarred from the beatings.

Noeli saw many recent marks and welts. She felt sorry for herself. she thought.

- Jesus! Why was that? Why were they hitting her?

- In one of my shows, the other clown hit me. It was supposed to be a lie, but to make it look original and so that I would actually scream, he actually hit me. I was also beaten for not wanting to do what I was told.

- So, what happened? How did you end up here?

- Noeli wanted to know.

- The circus was going to another town, this time further away, an eight-hour journey. I thought I should take advantage of this opportunity and planned to run away. I had very little money. I took advantage of the hard work involved in dismantling the circus to go to the train station in the afternoon, buy a ticket for twenty-three hours and to a town in the opposite direction to where the circus was going. I went south, while they went north. I took some of my clothes, put them in this backpack and left without anyone noticing. I traveled for five hours by train. When I got off, I went to the highway, got a ride and stopped at the road that goes down that way - he waved his hand towards the north.

The same place, the same entrance to the town where Antônio came from, thought Noeli.

He paused, took a drink of water and continued.

- I was drawn here. I don't know why I thought I'd find a luxurious house here. I was disappointed when I saw a ruin.

- This house was once an important manor house.

- A long time ago? - He asked.

- About fifty years.

- So that's why it's old like that!

Although this place looks different, I found it familiar. I knew where I was going, where the doors were. It was a familiar meeting! Do you understand?

- No - Noeli was laconic.

- Neither do I! Well... the fact is that I hadn't eaten since yesterday afternoon. That's why I was hungry. Thank you very much! Can't I stay here? As your servant? I work for food and a place to live.

- You'd better not.

- I have nowhere else to go! - he said sadly.

- Do you remember your mother?

- Very little. Sometimes I remember her holding me. She used to make me grow up. Let me stay here tonight, I'm tired. Where will I sleep? I don't have any money.

Noeli looked at him and remembered her vision.

João Luiz! Did the vision want to show me that João Luiz would come back? How I wish I understood. I'll let him stay tonight.

- You will sleep in the living room tonight, said the woman who lived in the house. - The rooms are closed, dirty and damp because of the leaks. I'll heat up some water so you can have a bath. It's dirty and smelly. I'll also make an herbal poultice for you to put on your back. I've run out of food. I gave you, my dinner. I live here alone and I'm so poor.

- Thank you, lady of the manor.

- Why did you say that?

- I don't know, it just popped into my head, he replied.

- Manor house is a big house, and this one is. I'd really like to have a bath, but I don't have any clean clothes. Can I wash the clothes in my backpack and my coat?

- Yes, you'd better stay hidden. Won't the circus people come after you?

- I don't think so. Maybe they'll only notice I'm missing when they organize the first show. They'll think I stayed in the town we were in. They won't come after me. I'm far away from them.

-Where did you sleep in the circus? - Noeli wanted to know.

- In an old lion cage. It wasn't locked.

The cage was under a tent. The circus always went to warmer places, we always had summer.

He went to wash his clothes and Noeli went to her room. She took a pair of pajamas she'd gotten from Pérola, which she felt were masculine, and cut a piece of fabric off the legs and arms.

It'll look good on him! she thought. He washed the clothes properly.

- Tomorrow, he said, I'll put these on clean and wash the ones I'm wearing. What's your name?

- Noeli.

- I heard someone call you Sofia, he said.

- It's a long story! My real name is Noeli which became Noeli; because they find it difficult and because I'm ugly and weird, they call me Stranger and also Sofia, because it's easier. I'll light the fire to heat up some water for you to bathe in, and you can apply this plaster to your wounds, put on these clean pajamas. I'll make a place for you to sleep in this corner of the room.

- Thank you very much! Can I fry some eggs and have them with bread for dinner? - he asked.

- Yes.

After his bath and with clean pajamas, he looked much better. They had dinner and went to bed early.

The next day, he put on his damp clothes and, after having breakfast, went to wash the rest of his clothes. There were only a few pieces.

- Do you only have these clothes? - she asked.

- Yes, at the circus I used to dress up as a clown all the time. The owner said that people liked to see me dressed like that. I didn't bring them; I want to forget that I worked as a clown. What can I do for you? I can look after the chickens. I can weed the garden.

You really helped her. They had lunch and went to clean the house.

- You use this bathroom; I keep using the other one.

- Where's the furniture in this house? I remember... You must have had a lot, right?

- I kept selling. Necessity made me sell, replied Noeli.

- Why don't you call me Pingo or Espirro?

- I don't like nicknames. Can I call you by a name?

- Yes, you can, he agreed.

- I'll call you João Luiz.

- I like it, it's a familiar name. It seems I've been called that before.

João Luiz and Noeli together again! thought Noeli. But what am I thinking? How absurd! But that's how I feel: together again!

# Chapter 6

## *BOTH IN THE MANOR HOUSE*

João Luiz helped his hostess clean the house, the kitchen and the vegetable garden.

- I wonder what people will think when they see him here. He seems happy. What should I do? What should I do? thought Noeli indecisively.

- Do I really have to hide? - asked João Luiz.

- I wanted to replant the cabbage bed.

- People might comment on it when they see it here. Then, I'm being honest, I can't support him. Sometimes I don't have enough to eat.

- Yes, you do! There are chickens, eggs and vegetables!

- They're new to you, you'll soon get sick of eating just that, replied Noeli.

- I've been through many needs; I think they were worse than hunger. You respect me, so much so that you refused to call me by a nickname, you gave me a name. I'm sure you're incapable of humiliating or beating me. If you go hungry, we'll go hungry together. Then, with me working, we'll earn more.

- Don't kid yourself, it won't be much. In this town, the houses have backyards, many of the residents keep chickens and have vegetable gardens.

- Please let me stay, he pleaded. - I don't want to end up in another circus, showing off my physical handicap. If I liked being a clown, if I had talent, it would be different, but I never did. I dreamed of farming for a living. Why do you fear comments? Do you worry about what people will think?

- I didn't have to worry about that. Comments bother me. People are mean.

- Don't you have any relatives so we can say I'm his son? A nephew or a close cousin?

- João Luiz asked.

- I'm an only child. I had two uncles, my mother's brothers, who left home and never returned. Will it work to say that you are the son of one of them? Would they believe this lie?

- We can tell them that I'm the son of one of your uncles who came here after his grandmother and aunt and found you - João Luiz got excited. - Tell us more about them, tell us everything you know about your uncles. I really want to stay here. Please!

Noeli told him everything she knew.

- I could be Zezinho's son. That's it! My father was Zezinho, the son of Maria and Antonieto, Mr. Nieto and Violeta's brother. It's a charitable lie. If you agree, I can say that I have a family, and that's important to me. I don't know the name of my mother or father.

- Sofia! Sofia! - Nalva shouted at the gate. João Luiz ran to answer her.

-Good morning! - he greeted happily. - My name is João Luiz, I'm related to Noeli Sofia. I'm Aunt Violeta's brother's son, my father was Grandma Maria and Grandpa Nieto's son. Pleased to meet you! What do you want?

- How did you end up here? - Curious, the neighboring customer wanted to know.

- My father had the address, he always talked about here and when he died, I was left alone. So, I came here.

João Luiz answered her and she bought eggs. And, as Noeli had predicted, the traffic increased. Nalva told her the news, and the neighboring shoppers, curious, came to meet the dwarf who was related to the Stranger, and João Luiz continued to explain:

- My father always talked about his parents, my grandparents.

I was left motherless and, when my father died, I decided to look for the only relatives I had. I found Noeli, I asked to stay, I'm going to help her with her work. I have few clothes. Don't you have any that I could use? We were poor, but honest and hardworking.

When he traveled, he only brought a few things, he couldn't bear the weight of too many.

In the afternoon, he got dinner ready and lots of clothes.

- They're children, but they're fine. You're going to let me stay here, aren't you? We won't be two lonely people any more. We can help each other.

- I'm still undecided, replied Noeli. He went into the bathroom, and Noeli saw her grandmother Maria.

- Granddaughter dear, said Maria, events can surprise us. God allows us to learn to love through reunions. I might like him as a grandson. João Luiz is a good name. If you want my opinion, let him stay.

- Grandma, what about Mom? - Noeli asked in thought. - How is she?

- My Violeta is fine, healthy, beautiful, just very homesick and very worried about you. She'll come to see you as soon as possible. God rest her soul!

The vision disappeared as João Luiz entered the kitchen.

- Shall we have dinner? Then I'll try on the clothes. If they don't fit, we'll donate them to those poor children who live on the other side. Don't you have a radio here?

- I don't have a radio, there's never been any money left over to buy one.

- Leave it to me, I'll order one, he said.

- Don't do that. I don't pay for the light. Mr. Danilo, a generous man who always helps me, pulled a wire from his house so we could have three light bulbs. I don't like to push it.

- How you've changed! Have I changed too? Don't abuse me!

- I really don't like to abuse. But why are you saying that? Be honest and explain it to me, she asked.

- I think we're always changing, and it's good that it's for the better. Maybe we've been worse.

- I don't understand.

- Have you ever heard of reincarnation? - João Luiz asked. - A theory, a story, that our spirit comes back in different physical bodies?

- Isn't that a legend? - asked Noeli.

- I don't think so. I'd even like to understand more about it. For a while, a couple of French artists worked in the circus. Their daughter, Marcelle, taught French to me and to Gracia, a friend. This French family believed in this fact and I started to think about it a lot and ask myself: Why was I born like this? Why am I so afraid of stairs? Why am I a dwarf? If God is good, why did he make me a dwarf? Was it injustice or justice? The answer I received in my heart, in my inner self, was: I'm sure I made a lot of mistakes, I didn't go to eternal hell, but, through God's goodness, I had the opportunity for my spirit to reincarnate, that is, to return again in a fleshly body that I deserved and to learn not to do evil anymore.

João Luiz sighed and looked at Noeli. They were both silent for a moment, then he spoke again:

- I can only believe in God if I believe in reincarnation. I can't even accept the idea that God made me a dwarf because he wanted to, that I should conform to his will.

- I think I have a lot to think about too. The possibility hadn't even crossed my mind.

- It's fair, don't you think? - João Luiz asked.

- I'm beginning to think so. My life isn't easy either. I'm ugly, strange, disabled, I'm alone in this house and I think I'm her.

- Her who? - João Luiz asked.

- The lady of the manor. The former owner of this place.

- Do you see glimpses of the past? You don't have to hide it from me. I understand. I'd like to understand better. If you feel you were someone else in the distant past, I'm not surprised, because I feel it too. Sometimes I see myself differently, tall, slender, riding imposingly on beautiful horses. The worst thing is when I see myself like this, I feel like I raped, punished and humiliated simple people, thinking that these people were my employees. When the man who gave me, a lift dropped me off at the entrance to the town, I knew exactly where I had to go. I seemed to be a magnet being attracted to metal. Only I thought I'd find a glorious house here and I saw the ruin. Have I been here before? Mystery! That's why, Noeli, I need to believe in reincarnation. If I was arrogant, proud, humiliated people I thought were inferior, in this life I was the inferior who received a lot of abuse, I was humiliated and, as the French couple said, it's not punishment, but learning through pain, because I refused to learn through love.

João Luiz left the kitchen, and Noeli wondered.

My God, does this justice exist? If reincarnation is real, I feel loved by God and not abandoned. To think with certainty that the Heavenly Father loves me is comforting, consoling. Perhaps I have been the Noeli of the past and have returned to the same place where I made so many mistakes, but very differently, and I have no longer been allowed to commit the abuses of yesteryear. My past actions are the result of the present I live in. I'll tell João Luiz that he can stay. He still has no memories of the place, but my guest used to come here to visit. Poor guy, he must have suffered for the mistakes he made. Was it a coincidence that I had that vision in which I made a lot of mistakes, I didn't go to eternal hell, but, through God's goodness, I had the opportunity for my spirit to reincarnate, that is, to return again in a fleshly body that I deserved and to learn not to do evil anymore?

One day, when they were in the library, João Luiz noticed that Noeli was struggling to read the book she had in her hands and asked:

- Why don't you wear reading glasses?

- Because I don't have any.

- Then get one...

- If I can't afford food, how can I afford glasses?

- You really get paid very little for your work. We need to think of another way of earning money. Ever since your plaster cured my wounds, I've been interested in the medicines you make. I think that with them, you'll be able to help more people and receive help in return. Rich people have physical pain too. Can I offer your plasters and remedies to the customers?

- Yes, you can, agreed Noeli.

João Luiz, however, wouldn't stay quiet for long and soon interrupted her reading again.

- Have you read all the books on the shelves?

- No, there are some that are written in other languages.

- Can I see them? - he asked. - Please let me, I'll be careful. Gracia had private tutors to teach her literacy and she demanded that I have lessons with her; that's why I know a little English, and Marcelle taught us French. Can I see them?

-Yes, we'll go and see them tomorrow after lunch. So, João Luiz, early in the morning, attending to the customers, offered the medicines and explained:

- Sofia Noeli doesn't charge for them, but we'll take them if you want to pay. To make them, she buys various things and, at the moment, these ingredients are missing. Dona Nalva - he smiled at his neighbor - your soup is a delicacy of the gods. So, you make it every Wednesday? Wouldn't you make some extra? I could get it.

At lunchtime, he told his hostess.

- Every Wednesday, I'll pick up our dinner at Mrs. Nalva's; on Sunday, lunch at Mrs. Celeida's; on Saturday, at Mrs. Ângela's; and?

- João Luiz, what did you do?

- I just wanted to pick it up. Don't you think it's very comfortable to receive at home? Those who want to seek, ask. Haven't you ever gone to collect?

- No, she replied.

- That's the rest of the manor lady's pride! Asking is allowed, but you mustn't abuse it. You don't ask, you wait to be offered. You should learn to ask, seek and, once you've received, thank. Think: don't you ask out of pride? If you went hungry and didn't ask, you deserved it. Because those neighbors are good people who like to help. I'll get it and be grateful. We certainly won't go hungry.

- Maybe, thought Noeli, I'm being too proud. João Luiz is right, I've never asked and I dread the thought of having to beg. I must try not to be proud anymore.

The next day, after lunch, the two of them went to look at the bookshelves.

- Here are the ones I've already read, and in this section are the ones I'm about to read. On this shelf are the ones in another language, she explained, showing the books.

- Indeed, they are in another language, he said, after examining them. - In this part, they're in English and French; these seem to be in Hindi. How interesting! The one with the green cover, in English, is about plants. We should take a look, maybe it can help us with our medicines. Wow, look at this: Allan Kardec! I can translate: "le livre" is "the book". I don't know what that other word means. Here are some dictionaries. The ones we're interested in are the English ones and this French one. I'll explain who this author is. Allan Kardec, according to my French friends, wrote about reincarnation and many other interesting subjects. I'm going to try to read them: the one about plants and the one by

Kardec. To do this, I'm going to consult the English and French dictionaries.

- We'll be able to do that in the evening. Now we have to work, Noeli reminded her.

Angela came to buy eggs, brought a lady with her and explained that she was a cousin who was staying at her house. The woman, Fiorella, asked João Luiz a lot of questions, such as:

- Are you married?

- No, ma'am, I'm single, he replied.

- Don't you miss a woman; I mean a companion?

- No, ma'am, I'm castrated.

- Fiorella, please stop asking me these questions, asked Angela.

- Well, what's wrong with asking. You...

- Let's go!

Angela pulled her cousin away. João Luiz went to the other side of the garden.

I wonder what 'castrated' means? I'll look it up in the dictionary, thought Noeli, who overheard the conversation.

She entered the house, went to the study and took the dictionary from the bookshelf.

My God! Poor João Luiz! 'Castrated' means 'unable to reproduce'. 'Castrate' means 'to cut off or destroy the reproductive organs'.

In the evening, after dinner, they took the four books to the kitchen: two dictionaries, the one on plants and the one on Allan Kardec.

- Were you castrated?

- No, I was born that way. I think that, out of regret, I castrated myself and passed on this deficiency to my physique. It doesn't bother me anymore. I said this to that curious woman because I saw evil in her eyes, surely, she thought that the two of us could have a relationship.

- Unfortunately, there are people who see evil in everything - Noeli sighed.

- Most people judge people by what they're capable of. Shall we read the books? We can see from the pictures of these plants if we know any of them and, with the help of the dictionary, find out what it says about them.

As for the French book, I'm going to look up the meaning of this word, "mediums", because these, "le livre des", I know are "the book of"[6]. After looking it up, João Luiz exclaimed in annoyance:

- I can't find it. I think we'll have to read it and then maybe we'll understand what it means. I'll translate the text from the beginning and then the index.

- Isn't the word "mediums" something like "medium"?

- *"The book of Mediums"*? - João Luiz asked.

- It's too strange. Look up synonyms for "medium" in our language's dictionary.

Noeli did.

- There are many synonyms for the word "medium". Perhaps this one could define it better: "intermediary". And "intermediary" means "mediator". Maybe it's *"The book of the Mediums"*, those who stand between the dead and the living.

---

[6] N. A. E.: The edition that the two of them had in their hands had written on the cover *Le livre des médiums* or *guide des médiums et des évocateurs*, 15/01/1861.

Those who can feel, see and speak to those who live in another way.

- It makes sense, agreed João Luiz.

They both realized that the work would take a long time.

- Tell you what, decided Noeli. - I'll look for plants I know in the pictures, and you mark the words you don't know in pencil, and then I'll look them up in the dictionary. You do the same with this book by Allan Kardec. We'll work on them and then we'll finish the job.

The days for Noeli were no longer routine. João Luiz was cheerful and explained why.

- Although I'm sleeping in the corner of the room, it's better than in the lion's cage, I haven't been beaten anymore, my wounds have healed, I've been eating and, best of all, I'm learning how to make medicine. Speaking of medicines, when I was picking up the soup from Mrs. Nalva's house, I saw Rosiña saying that her father, Mr. Danilo, who you love so much and are grateful for, is sick with a urine infection. Why don't you take him some medicine?

- I don't usually offer it, said the resident of the manor house.

- I think you should take it, explain how to take it, and whether you take it or not is up to him. We'll put the medicine in this glass that we've boiled and make him pray to attract good energy so that this kind man can heal.

João Luiz eventually convinced her. They made the medicine, and Noeli made it, really wanting Danilo to heal. In the afternoon, she went to take him. Embarrassed to be offering, she knocked on the door and Olga welcomed her in.

- Mr. Danilo, she said when she saw him, I've come to visit you and I've brought this home remedy. My grandmother Maria used to make it, then my mother, and now I'm making it. This is for a urine infection. If you want to take it, I'm sure it will do you good, I made it with a lot of love.

- Yes, I will, said Danilo.

She explained how to use it and Danilo took the first dose in front of her. Noeli accepted the coffee and then said goodbye, wishing that he would heal soon.

Three days later, Rosiña went to report that her father had healed. Demand for the medicine increased.

João Luiz changed the manor resident's routine. He got a radio, asked Danilo if he could turn it on and, with his permission, the two of them started listening to music and the news. They now worked more on growing herbs.

The book on plants didn't help them, there were few they knew. They gave up. She started helping him with Allan Kardec's book.

- What's making it difficult is that I can't find some words in the French dictionary we have, João Luiz lamented. - I think that many of the words written in this book were created by the author to define these phenomena better. I will read the book from the beginning for you.[7] It contains the special teaching of the spirits on the theory of all kinds of manifestations, the means of communication with the invisible world, the development of mediumship, the difficulties and pitfalls that can be encountered in the practice

---

[7] N. A. E.: João Luiz certainly had a hard time translating, and he did so with some parts incomplete, others erroneous, but it gave them the valuable information they needed.

of Spiritism. "Mediumship" and "Spiritism", we don't know what they mean, but they must be important words.

Noeli consulted the dictionary of the language she was speaking, looked up the meaning of some words, and the two of them concluded: the book would help them understand the visions, the glimpses they had of the past.

- I think, João Luiz, that this book is the key to learning to live together, to understanding what is happening to us. Let's focus our study on this book, it will certainly change our lives.

# Chapter 7
## *THE MEDIUMS' BOOK*

Noeli's life was no longer as routine as before, although various tasks had to be done every day. Four days a week they didn't cook dinner, nor did they cook lunch on Saturday and Sunday, because João Luiz would get the food ready from the neighboring houses. The manor's new resident talked a lot, distracting her, and listening to the radio was a pleasure for her. The two of them made a lot of medicines and ointments to order. They didn't charge poor people or accept anything in return. After Danilo healed, people came from all over the city to get the medicines, and they received food, clothes and money for them.

- Didn't I say we wouldn't go hungry? - recalled João Luiz.

He liked meeting people and was called by his name; sometimes "short", and rarely "dwarf". When this happened, he didn't think it was a bad thing, he smiled endearingly and tried to remind the person that his name was João Luiz.

Every night they concentrated on translating Kardec's book. He translated, and Noeli looked up the words in the dictionary and wrote the text in a notebook. The index was ready.

- The subjects are really interesting! - she exclaimed. - Too bad this book doesn't talk about reincarnation. We're going to work on chapter XIV, the title of which is the word we haven't translated.

That evening, they translated item one hundred and fifty-nine.

- "Mediums"[8], then, are anyone who feels the influence of spirits, in any degree of intensity, concluded João Luiz.

- We're both mediums, exclaimed Noeli.

- Item one hundred and sixty-one says: involuntary or natural mediums are those who exert their influence unintentionally. Those who hear are "audients", those who see are "videtes".

João Luiz decided to go back to the beginning and, two weeks later, he concluded:

- We are spirits and we can live in different places, we are called "soul" when we are dressed in our physical body and "spirit" when we are on another plane. And mediums are the people who can feel them, see them, talk to them, to spirits.

The two of them worked hard during the day; they cut down on the vegetable beds and the chickens, and concentrated on making the medicines. At night they worked on translating *The Mediums' Book*.

- Although, said Noeli, we haven't yet found anything in this work about reincarnation, we can conclude that we are evolving and, for this, it is necessary to return several times to the physical plane; in these returns, we can be more sensitive and capture those who live on the spiritual plane. By understanding what happens to me, I can say that I'm not strange at all, but rather a normal being. This is gratifying to me. There must be many people like us who hide this fact so

---

[8] N. A. E.: Since they didn't translate it, they wrote and spoke the word in French.

as not to be called "witches" or worse, like me, who was nicknamed Stranger; people who are ashamed, suffer and cannot understand what is happening to them.

- Worse are those who are labeled mentally ill and taken to mental institutions, those who are obsessed.

- Knowing about this possibility would do a lot of people good, commented Noeli.

- I hope that this work, like the others by Mr. Allan Kardec, will be translated into many languages.

Perhaps it has already been in our language, but there aren't even any bookshops here...

The other day, João Luiz was pensive and when Noeli asked him why, he replied:

- I don't know if I'm baptized. I didn't even have a name. Is it true that pagans don't go to heaven?

- To believe that is to call God an executioner. Mr. Kardec would certainly reply that this law was invented by men and does not come from God. Does that bother you? Not being baptized?

- I'd like to believe not, but I have my doubts. I heard in the circus that I wasn't baptized and that I was an animal.

- There are worse people than animals, commented Noeli.

- If you want to be baptized, I can ask Father Ambrózio. He once told me that if I needed anything, I could ask him. Tomorrow we'll go to church at 3 p.m. By this time the priest has had lunch and had his siesta, and there's usually no one in church.

The next day they got ready, closed up the house and went to church. Father Ambrózio lived in a house next to the church and, as they didn't find him there, they went to his residence.

The priest greeted them with a smile.

- I'm so glad you came to see me, miss! I'm having a lot of stomach pains and I was even going to ask Angela to get me some medicine. What the doctor prescribed isn't working.

- It would be a pleasure to make some medicine for you. I came here because, a few years ago, you told me that if I needed you, I could come and, if I could, you would help me. We don't know if João Luiz is baptized, and he wants to be baptized. Don't you baptize him?

- I baptize everyone who asks, replied the priest.

- Then you can baptize him. Can it be now? - Noeli asked.

- I usually do it on Sundays, after Mass, replied Father Ambrózio.

- But you'll do it now, won't you? - she said.

- We dressed in our best clothes for the ceremony.

- You know that on Sunday we'll be in the way because everyone will be curious to see the stranger and the dwarf in the church.

- I don't mind and... - said João Luiz, who until that moment had been silent.

- It'll be like that, won't it, Father? - interrupted Noeli. - We'll go to the church and you can baptize him.

The priest agreed and they went to the church.

- Who are the godparents? - asked the priest.

- Godparents? - João Luiz asked, looking at Noeli.

- Me, of course, she replied, I've always wanted to be someone's godmother. Why don't you, João Luiz, ask Father Ambrózio to be your godfather?

- May I?

- You accept, don't you, Father? - Noeli asked, smiling.

- Okay, I accept. I'm not anyone's godfather either. This will be the first time. Let's go to the baptismal font!

In a simple ceremony, João Luiz was baptized.

Noeli gave him her surname. The three of them felt good, they were happy. They thanked the priest and said goodbye.

- That's it! - she exclaimed. - If I was a pagan, now I'm not.

- I don't feel any different, although I felt good about the ceremony. Doesn't the church charge for baptism?

- If it does, we don't pay. In return, I won't charge him for his medicine. Father Ambrózio is a good person, charitable and exercises his priesthood well. I feel good energy when I'm around him. At the ceremony, I saw a spirit dressed in a cassock who, by the light he radiated, is a kind being. Father Ambrózio doesn't charge the poor anything.

- Should I call you "godmother"? - he asked.

- No, keep calling me Noeli. In my heart, I think that baptism, an external act, serves no purpose. Perhaps the meaning of baptism is inner change for the better.

- If God really separates the baptized from the pagans, I'll be among the baptized! - João Luiz smiled happily.

- We've been born many times. How many times have I been baptized? Now you're baptized, you have godparents, and this question is settled.

- Gracia would be delighted to hear about my baptism! - João Luiz sighed.

- You talk about Gracia a lot. Do you love her?

- I loved her very much. When I went to the circus, Gracia was a baby, then a girl, and for a while we studied together, I became literate at her request.

Gracia defended me as best she could. She lived in a trailer with her parents and two brothers, all artists. I hid some of the bad things they did to me from her so as not to upset her. There was no way she could defend me against everything. Gracia shared the treats she got with me.

- Tell me about your life in the circus, Noeli asked.

- Talking about sadness on the day of my christening? No, I'm going to talk about Gracia. I'm really missing her today. She's beautiful. I haven't seen her for a long time. She's blonde, blue-eyed and very delicate. She used to work as an aerialist. She met a young man from another circus, who was much bigger. They dated more by correspondence, got married, and she left with him.

João Luiz sighed. Noeli realized that her godson had suffered a lot and was still suffering.

- You love her! - she exclaimed.

- I can't compare; I've loved two people to this day. Her, perhaps as a mother, sister and friend, and now I like you.

- But in a different way. Noeli thought of Antero.

There are many ways to love. I understand, João Luiz loved Gracia like I loved Antero. A platonic love, pure and intense. Perhaps he loved her more because he lived with her.

- You didn't see her after you got married?

- No, he answered. - Gracia only wrote me one letter. Sometimes she wrote to her parents and sent me hugs. It wasn't easy for us to correspond, we were always going from one city to another, and so was she. I pray to her every night that she'll be happy.

After that day, João Luiz went on to recount the events of his life. Noeli concluded that he would suffer a lot. Ever since he arrived at the circus, they dressed him up as a clown and taught him how to make merry. He was fed and only went hungry when everyone from the circus passed away.

First, he slept in a trailer with an old woman and, when she died, he went to the cage. Their life in the circus wasn't easy. In some towns they were accepted, in others they were not. They had to flee some because they were in debt. He didn't like being a performer, he was kicked, he was belted and, when they found out he was afraid of stairs, they made him climb them: he screamed, and the audience didn't even realize that his screams were actually terrified.

- The worst thing, he recounted one afternoon when they were redoing a flowerbed, was that the circus owner's son raped me, and those who knew laughed.

João Luiz cried. Noeli felt like hugging him to comfort him, but she didn't; she just said:

- This will pass...

- Thank God! - he exclaimed. - That's why I'm happy here. Thank you, Godmother, thank you very much. That's why I believe in reincarnation. I learned a lesson from what happened to me. Never again will I force anyone to do what they don't want to do. I'm always going to respect others: in their physical state, in their feelings and, if life puts me in a better position, I'll help people.

- You're already starting to prove that, said Noeli.

- Me?

- You treat everyone well, especially the poor people who come to collect their medicine, you play with the children and you don't mistreat anyone.

- I like children! - exclaimed João Luiz.

- You've learned to love them.

- I hope I never forget that, to love everyone.

- A lesson repeated is a lesson learned, said Violeta's daughter.

- God willing I'll learn!

- Have you tried to run away from the circus other times?

- Yes, he replied. - Once, after being sexually abused again, I took some clothes and ran away. As I hadn't planned it and had no money, I walked towards the outskirts and ended up in a farmhouse. The couple who lived there let me sleep in a shed and gave me food. The next day, the man took me, put me in a sack and tied me up. I was immobilized and in the dark. I heard the couple talking, and the man said to the woman: 'There's a reward for him, the circus owner has offered money to whoever takes him back. I'll go into town, hand him over, get the reward, go to the store and buy some food. I realized that they had put me in a cart and we soon arrived. The circus owner opened the bag, took me out, put me in the cage and locked it. He paid the man. I was watched for a while and locked in the cage every night. I didn't try to escape again; I didn't want to be away from Gracia and also because the son of the circus owner who raped me got married and left me alone. This time, I planned my escape, and it worked. I no longer had any reason to stay in the circus after Gracia left.

In the evening João Luiz showed Noeli.

- Look at this page in Allan Kardec's book. Someone has written next to it. It's in chapter twenty-three, "Obsession". I managed to translate what this word is. What I understand is: the domination that certain spirits can acquire over certain people. And when this happens, it is always inferior spirits who seek to dominate. Good spirits, who were good people when they were incarnate, do not exert these constraints; kind beings advise and combat the influence of the evil ones.

She picked up the book and saw something on the inside of the page, written in fountain pen, that she felt was written by Pietro. She read aloud what was written:

- I must have been obsessed. I've certainly done things while subjugated. It can only be this. I need help. I must seek help. - Noeli asked: - Is this possible?

- Let's think about it: if there are good and bad people here on Earth, they must remain good and bad when they die. That must be why the heir to this manor went on a journey in search of help. I looked in the book for the word "subjugated" and found "subjugation" in chapter twenty-three. Listen: "It's an involvement that paralyzes the victim's will, making them act in spite of themselves. The victim is under a real yoke, which can be moral or corporeal".[9]

- Does it have any more marked pages or other writings? - Noeli asked.

---

[9] N. A. E.: This book is really interesting. I invite the reader to look it over.

- I looked for it and didn't find anything else written, but I did find a text crossed out; it's at the end, in the last paragraph, and I translated it, listen, I'm going to read it: Indeed, the ease with which certain people accept everything that comes from the invisible world under the cover of a great name is what encourages mystifying spirits. We must apply all our attention to unraveling the plots of these spirits, but we can only do this with the help of experience, acquired through serious study. That's why we keep repeating: Study before you practice, because that's the only way you won't have to acquire experience at your own expense.

- What a beautiful teaching! - Noeli exclaimed with emotion. - This book really is a masterpiece. Let's keep studying, shall we?

- Yes, let's go, said João Luiz. - The conclusion I've drawn from what we've studied so far is: there are more sensitive people who mediate. While we live in the body of flesh, we are on the physical plane, we are incarnate, and when this body dies, we live in another way, disincarnate, and the sensitive ones can communicate with those in the afterlife. Allan Kardec calls these people mediums. Spirits are good and bad, and in order to be in tune with the good ones, we have to be good.

- There are also people who don't forgive and who can take revenge after they die.

- They really can! - he exclaimed, sighing. - From what I understand, Mr. Pietro was obsessed by a spirit, or more than one, who was persecuting him.

This happened to me. I'll tell you about it. At the time it happened, I didn't understand; now, with the reading of this book, I'm beginning to understand. I remember that, as a child, I had nightmares and, when I went to the circus, I heard the laughter of someone invisible, and the nightmares continued. When I was raped for the first time, I was in the cage bruised, very unhappy, and I cried a lot. Then I saw the figure of a woman's spirit; this time she didn't laugh, her eyes sparkled, she didn't speak, but I heard her. Now I conclude that this spirit hated me, it was taking revenge, she thought, and I understood her.

She gave me the message: Where is the rich man? The arrogant one who used people? Did you enjoy being raped? You did this to me and you didn't care about my suffering. That's why it's no longer worth seeing you suffer. I'm going to mind my own business. I'll leave you in hell, because your rapist enjoyed it and will do it again, just like you did to me. Stay with the devil! Goodbye!. The vision, this spirit, disappeared, and I no longer had nightmares or felt, saw or heard it. This spirit, this woman, didn't forgive me and took her revenge. I must have really hurt her, who, instead of getting on with her life, stopped to make me suffer. When she felt avenged, she left, perhaps even reincarnated or moved to a place where spirits live. After reading this book, I began to think about my actions, what I have done and what I have received. I concluded, while praying the Our Father, that we must forgive in order to be truly forgiven. I have managed to forgive everyone: my father, the stepmother who sold me, those who mistreated me at the circus and the man who raped me. I don't want to be hurt and I've even been able to pray for them. By doing so, I can ask for forgiveness.

- How can you ask for forgiveness if you don't know who your victims are, whether they are dressed in their fleshly bodies or not? - asked the resident of the manor house.

- But God knows that I have forgiven and that I have asked for forgiveness! Those who mistreated me didn't ask for forgiveness either, and yet I forgave them.

- In this life, existence, I have nothing to forgive or ask for forgiveness. Some people tried to offend me when they called me Strange and Ugly, but I understood and I wasn't hurt. I'm going to do as you do and ask for forgiveness. I'm sure I'll receive reactions to my wrongdoings, and wrongdoings are wrongs committed. But what if someone doesn't want to forgive?

- I think that's their problem, replied João Luiz.

- Not forgiving is wrong, because not forgiving is not being forgiven. That's why I pray so much for those who have mistreated me and for those I have mistreated. I have felt peace with this attitude.

From that day on, Noeli prayed more and asked God to forgive her; that if she had made victims, that they would forgive her.

Every night they both prayed together, then they worked on the translation, which became easier as they got to know the words better.

- How I'd like to be part of a meeting of mediums, exclaimed Noeli.

- Me too. Maybe there are some in the area. There aren't any in this city; if there were, I'd know about it. I've been speculating, I even asked Father Ambrózio, but he doesn't know anything about it, he told me he'd never heard of Allan Kardec.

- The mediums who have the privilege of doing good with this sensitivity, of being part of a group, of studying together, don't know the grace they are receiving. It is a valuable gift to help others, both those on the physical plane and those on the spiritual plane. If I receive this gift in my next incarnation, I will be very grateful.

The atmosphere in the manor got better, and Noeli no longer had visions of Noeli, no more flashes of her past. However, she certainly felt that she had been the former mistress of the manor and João Luiz the lover from the past, Thomas' nephew/son. God is so good! What an opportunity to learn.

They made a lot of medicines, shared tasks, and he was the one who went out to do the shopping, collect the food they earned and deliver the medicines, as well as going to church and taking medicines to Father Ambrózio.

- I like going to church and talking to my godfather.

I like him!

Father Ambrózio gave him presents, almost always clothes.

And the days were quiet.

# Chapter 8

## *ALONE AGAIN*

One morning, the two residents of the old manor house were working on a bed of herbs. João Luiz smiled.

- Why are you smiling? - asked Noeli.

- Today is Gracia's birthday, she's twenty-eight.

- So, you're thirty-six?

- That must be it.

- When's your birthday? - she asked.

- I don't know.

- It could be today! I can bake you a cake!

- A party? - João Luiz was thrilled. - No one has ever greeted me for my birthday. Can I invite people?

- To eat a simple cake?

- If you let me, I'll manage the party. I can't do it today, there's not much time. Tomorrow will be my birthday, I'll be thirty-six. How I wish Gracia knew that my birthday is now.

How he loved her, thought Noeli, he still does. Love feeds life!

Soon after, the first customer arrived, and João Luiz, all cheerful, invited her in:

- Dona Nalva, tomorrow is my birthday, I'm thirty-six. I've never had a party, and Noeli is going to bake me a cake. I want to invite you to come and eat it with us tomorrow at four o'clock. We'll just have a simple cake, a small slice for each of us. The party is just to sing Happy Birthday.

As expected, Nalva accepted the invitation and said:

- I'll bring some sweets.

And first thing in the morning, she had already got refreshments and snacks, and Celeida would make the cake. After lunch, he went to the houses of other neighbors and customers to invite them and also invited his godfather.

João Luiz planned everything; enthusiastically, he pleased the woman who lived in the house.

The next day, at 15:30, everything was ready and they were both well dressed. At the party, there was plenty, everyone came; João Luiz cried when they sang the song wishing him well.

The guests enjoyed the party. Father Ambrózio didn't go; he said that if it was his birthday, he would have to go to all the parties he was invited to, but he would give him a present.

The birthday boy got lots of presents: warm clothes and new clothes.

- This is the first time I'll be wearing clothes that haven't been worn! Look at this shirt! It's beautiful! - he exclaimed happily.

The guests left, the last at 17:30.

- As I predicted, there was a lot left over. Help me, Noeli: let's set the table again; at eighteen o'clock the children from the next street will arrive.

- What? Did you invite them? - Noeli was surprised.

- Yes, I invited them. The store owner gave me two packets of sweets and a large one of candies: I'll put them on the table with what's left. I'll have another party, and this one will be more interesting. Perhaps, like me, those children had never had a birthday party or been to one.

It was again very pleasant: mothers and children came, sang and ate everything there was. To brighten up the room, Noeli lit candles in addition to a lamp, and the children enjoyed themselves.

When everyone left, they closed up the house and cleaned it.

- Thank you, godmother! It was a very happy day! It's a pity I can't celebrate my birthday more often each year. Next year, I'll have another party. You let me, don't you? Do you know what gift I liked the most? First: your smile, you smiled all the time at both parties. I noticed! Second: the joy of the children; they ate sweets, had refreshments, sang, it was great. And third: they sang to me. I liked being greeted.

João Luiz has really changed! she thought. For someone who used to despise the poor, he now enjoys their company.

- Let's pray, invited the birthday boy. - I want to thank you for the happy day I've had. Then I'm going to pick the two herbs for Mrs. Nalva's medicine and I'm going to find my own corner to sleep in. Did you hear Angela say that winter will be harsh this year? It's a good thing I got a coat and a sweater.

After the prayer, Noeli went to her room.

She sat down on her bed; she was happy. She felt a different energy, looked at the bed next to her and saw her grandmother and mother.

- Mommy! - she exclaimed with emotion.

- Darling daughter! I've come for the party! I'm glad to see you happy, I'm feeling well too. Why is the bed empty?

- Granddaughter, said Maria, as I promised, I've brought Violeta to visit you, she'll go back to her new home with peace of mind knowing that you're all right. The party's over, let's go. As always, I'll be here. Stay with God!

The visions disappeared. Noeli, overcome with emotion, wiped away her tears.

- Thank you, God, thank you! She touched her hand where she saw her mother sitting.

Mom asked why it's empty. I wonder what she meant. My mommy looks so beautiful! I saw her healthy teeth when she smiled; she's flushed and looks younger. I felt that she was well. I'm so glad I got to see her!

She didn't cry, as she thought she would when she saw her mother. Hearing João Luiz's noise in the living room, she went in.

- Angela asked me about the expensive objects in the house. What happened to them? - João Luiz asked.

- I sold them until they ran out. A rich lady used to buy them. I sold everything I could, and only the paintings in the living room remained, because I decided not to get rid of the ones on the stairs, and then I thought that no one would want to buy portraits. Shortly after I sold the last items, my mother died, and so did Mrs. Pérola, the buyer. Her husband was ill; she appeared healthy, suffered a heart attack and died.

- If you want, I can try to sell these paintings - João Luiz offered.

- You can try: if you succeed, sell them. I've yet to give you, my present. Do you know what that will be? If you want, you can sleep in my room.

- What? - He asked in surprise, opening his mouth.

- In my room, there are two beds with good mattresses, and you can sleep on the one that used to belong to Mom. There's no point in you sleeping on the floor in the living room. In fact, a harsh winter is forecast. So, do you accept?

- Oh my God! That's a lot of joy for one day. I was afraid to sleep in this corner of the room. It was the best present. Thank you! Thank you!

He quickly went to his room.

-Tomorrow, I'll give you the mattress I used to sleep on. I got it from Angela; it's fine, but this is better.

They got ready for bed. As they lay there, he commented:

- Having the light of the candle is very good. I think it's the first time I've slept in a bed. How nice! Godmother, shall we agree on something? You never had a father, so I'll be your father. The adoptive father of the heart. And from now on, you'll be my mommy. I'll be father and son to you, and you'll be my mother and daughter. Father Ambrózio told me that the purest and most intense feeling is maternal and paternal. It is this feeling that we will nurture for each other. We won't talk about it with anyone; for everyone else, I'll continue sleeping in the living room. I'm going to thank God! Shall we pray again?

They prayed and slept peacefully.

Then they slept in the same room, and the affection between them grew stronger. They no longer felt afraid; each one gave the other security.

João Luiz sold the paintings in the living room and Noeli thought he had made a good sale. She kept the money because inflation was low.

It's good to keep this money. It's a guarantee. I'll use it when I need it, she said.

The residents of the manor had a quiet few days, always trying to help those who asked for help.

Early in the morning, Nereide, Cida's daughter, shouted at the gate:

- Sofia, João Luiz, I want to ask you a huge favor. As you know, I have five children, we live in a small house with three rooms, and we've had a lot of difficulties. My husband is a hard worker, he works on a farm, earns little and likes to drink. I got pregnant again. I need an abortion drug.

Please make it for me. How can I have another child?

The residents of the manor looked at each other. Noeli answered:

- I don't know how to do that. I really don't!

- Don't think about having an abortion, João Luiz begged. - I'm going to help you have another child. Please don't have an abortion! If God said it, God will take care of it! I'm going to ask you for help.

He started immediately, asking everyone he knew to help Nereide. Father Ambrózio went to her house, talked to the couple and advised her husband to stop drinking. She got the baby's trousseau, clothes for the other children, mattresses, household utensils and toys.

When the baby was born, Nereide came to show her son to the residents of the manor.

- I want to thank you, look what a beautiful child! The doctor operated on me so I wouldn't get pregnant again. With this child, our life has improved. My husband's boss now gives me part of his salary in food, and he's drinking less after Father Ambrózio talked to us.

When the two of them were alone, Noeli asked her godson:

- Who do you think this spirit is who was born into a family with so many problems and so poor?

- Surely, he is someone in need of learning, as we all are, or a friendly spirit who came to help the family, to be close to affection. Surely, he was afraid of being aborted. Do you know how to make abortion medicine?

- I know, but I don't do it, replied Noeli.

- When you know, it can be a temptation, concluded João Luiz. - You did the right thing. Even with my disability, I'm grateful to be reincarnated. I certainly suffered a lot on the spiritual plane. Do you think that if I die now, I will suffer?

- Absolutely not! What are we doing wrong?

We are doing good.

- I hope that the "thank you" and "God repay you" we hear are blessings to light our way in the afterlife.

They laughed and went to take their medicine.

One afternoon, a neighbor from across the street shouted at the gate:

- Sofia! João Luiz! My brother has been stabbed. It happened yesterday in a bar, in a fight. The doctor saw him, bandaged him up and he's in a lot of pain.

The two of them took some painkillers to help him heal and went to the wounded man. On seeing him, Noeli concluded:

- It's starting to fester. We have to clean the wound.

For days, the two of them visited the injured man, bringing medicine and bandages.

- When I see you two coming in here - said the young man

- I see lights together and I feel better. I've been wondering why you do this? Is it out of kindness? I've decided to be a better person with your example. I'll be a good son; I won't go to bars or get drunk anymore. Should I thank you?

- Yes, of course, replied João Luiz. - It's always good to say thank you. You feel good when you do.

- So, thank you very much. I won't call you Stranger or Dwarf anymore.

They both smiled. On their way home, Noeli commented:

- I think many people refer to us by the adjectives "stranger" and "dwarf". I don't mind. Do you?

- I don't mind either. I'm a dwarf, but you're not strange. It's so good that God allowed us to meet again. Because I feel like it wasn't a meeting, but a reunion. And we do good together. Isn't that wonderful?

- It certainly is! - Noeli exclaimed happily.

- The good we do makes us happy, because in doing it, we do it to ourselves first, he said.

The two of them dedicated themselves more to making medicines, plasters and ointments, which were sold, exchanged and donated to the poor. The vegetable garden was small, more for their own consumption; the chickens provided eggs, which were still sold. João Luiz used to get ready-made food from neighbors' houses a few days a week.

He talked a lot and made many friends. For three years, they celebrated his birthday with two parties. They both finished the translation of *The Mediums' Book* and always read the notes, as well as the Gospels that were in the Bible; they prayed together every night and slept peacefully. Although Noeli felt muscle pain, she didn't complain, she was fine.

- João Luiz and I learned to love each other with fraternity. We've reconciled and love each other like close relatives. This is gratifying, Noeli always thought.

They both lacked nothing. João Luiz collected clothes and food and distributed them to the poor across the street. He was a sweetheart.

- Godmother - I called her that when they were alone - I had three phases in my life. The first, I remember very little, was on the farm with my parents. The second was one of suffering, humiliation, a rescue through pain. The third, in the old manor house, was when I learned that we can pay off our debts by doing good. I'm happy here!

- I also feel good with you!

Noeli didn't have any more visions with Noeli, or now she understood that they were stories from her past. She always saw her grandmother Maria, and she was always helping to make the medicine. She also saw her mother.

- I'm fine, child, said Violeta. - It's important for all of us to live incarnate for the planned time. One day you'll be living with us - and she would give us advice: "Put this plaster on your foot properly!", "Eat well!"; "Don't be lazy about washing your hair like I used to!" etc.

Olga died and Noeli and João Luiz went to the wake.

She worried about her neighbor, saw that he was suffering and tried to comfort him. When they got home, João Luiz commented:

- Do you know what I want to do when I die and I'm over there?

- Grow up, get tall, replied Noeli.

- If that's possible, fine. I don't think I'll need to be a dwarf on the spiritual plane, but if I continue, I won't mind, I've got used to my height. But you made a mistake. The first thing I'll do, if possible, is see Gracia. It will be an exciting reunion! She certainly won't see me. She'll be older, maybe fat, but not ugly. No one is ugly to someone they love.

- I thought you'd want to see your mother.

- Hasn't she already been reincarnated? Of course, I'll want to know about her and I hope to see her all right.

- Would you help your father and stepmother? - Noeli wanted to know.

- If they need it and I can, I'll help them, yes. Godmother, have you ever thought that we are helped and have been helped and that, perhaps, among these people, there is someone we have harmed? A former enemy? Isn't that wonderful? With our attitudes, we can turn disaffection into affection. Life gives us opportunities to reconcile.

- That's a fact! she thought. Of course, I was the former owner of the manor, and João Luiz, my lover, who blamed me for his death. I feel like we were both in the past. Now he loves me. If my godson hears about this, will he still be my friend? Should I tell him or not? What if I'm wrong? It's best not to.

The important thing is that we become affectionate. What about me? Will I want to see Antero again? I don't think so. I'm really going to hug Grandma and Mom.

Three months after this conversation, it was four years since João Luiz had been living in the manor house.

That night, there was a storm and, the next morning, when Noeli went to the bathroom, she saw that one of the corners of the house had collapsed, flooding the room.

- I'm going to take advantage of the rain so I can get up on the roof and fix this gap so it won't drip anymore, said João Luiz.

- How are you going to get up there?

- Up the tree.

- Isn't it better to go up the ladder? - asked Noeli. - It's old, but it's in one piece. It can bear your weight.

- Me? Climb the ladder? No way! I'll climb the tree!

The two of them went out into the yard and planned what they would do.

- I'll climb the tree by these branches, he said, until I reach the edge of the roof. I'm not afraid of heights, just ladders. I put the tiles in place and then climb down.

- Can the branches support your weight?

- I weigh little, I'm light. The tree is green, I don't see a problem.

He climbed up, and Noeli stayed below, watching. Cleverly, João Luiz moved from one branch to another. Suddenly, they heard a snap, the branch broke and he fell. She ran and tried to catch him, but couldn't. Her godson fell on top of the broken branch, which entered his back, causing a point to appear on his chest.

- Noeli... Godmother... I fell! - he said softly and added: - Grandma Maria!

For a moment, the manor resident didn't know what to do. He looked at her and tried to smile. Noeli picked him up, but didn't move the branch; she remembered what the young man who had died in the house said: "If I take the knife out, I'll bleed". She put him on her lap and walked as fast as she could to Danilo's house. She thought she had fainted, but her godson had passed away. She didn't even notice that she was covered in blood, as it was pouring out of the wounded man's back.

When she got close to Danilo's house, she shouted for him and, frightened, he came to the door.

- Help us, Mr. Danilo! João Luiz has been hurt!

When Danilo saw them, he shouted for his grandson and the two of them quickly got him into the car. They went to the hospital, which had recently opened; it was small, but the population was happy with it. The resident of the manor house didn't know him. The car stopped, Danilo's grandson helped her down, and the kind neighbor accompanied her. As soon as they got in, two nurses put the wounded man on a stretcher, called the emergency room, and the doctor on duty ordered him to be taken to the operating room.

Danilo made his neighbor sit down and stood next to him. She called out for help, asking God, Jesus and her grandmother Maria to help her friend. The two of them, Danilo and Noeli, remained seated and silent.

About fifteen minutes passed and a nurse came into the hallway. At a signal, she called Danilo, who got up and went to talk to her. He returned, sat down again next to Noeli, took her bloodstained hand and spoke:

- Miss, you have to be strong! Your friend's wound was very serious. He must have died as soon as he fell. I think God took him to a better life.

Noeli couldn't say anything, she just stared at her neighbor. Why, my God? Why another loss? she thought.

-Miss, Danilo continued, we should go to your house so that you can change your clothes.

She then looked down at her skirt, it was soaked with blood, the liquid had run down her legs.

- I don't know what to do... - she managed to say.

- I'll take you home, you get cleaned up, change, get some clothes for João Luiz, and we'll come back here, I'll help you.

- You're an angel that God put in my life! Did João Luiz really die? Are you sure? Can't the doctor save him?

- Miss, death is something we don't understand yet. We know that when we are born, we will die one day. Everyone has their own time. João Luiz has died. The nurse told me that he arrived at the hospital dead, that his injury was very serious and that he wouldn't survive. Go ahead! Feel God with you! I have to help you make the arrangements.

- Mr. Danilo, this time I have money, I sold some paintings from the house. I think it will cover the cost of the funeral.

- I have very little money at the moment! - Danilo sighed. - When my Olga died, her children decided to divide up everything we had, and one of them is taking care of my money.

Danilo wiped away some tears. Noeli looked at him with pity.

Mr. Danilo has aged a lot with his widowhood. He must miss Mrs. Olga very much. How sad that his children should do this to him, share his material possessions and control his spending.

The two of them went to the car, his grandson was waiting for them; they got into the vehicle. She saw that the back seat was dirty with blood.

- I've made a mess of the car! - she exclaimed.

- It's all right, at home I'll ask the maid to clean it up, said Danilo. - I'll leave you at the manor house.

When you're ready, come to my house and I'll take you back to the hospital. You'll leave João Luiz's clothes for him to wear to the wake. Then we'll go to the funeral home and then to the cemetery.

At home, Noeli took out the money she had saved and counted it. I hope this money will cover the expenses.

I'm going to change, there's no time to heat water for the bath.

She was very dirty. She took off her clothes, wiped herself with the towel, changed and soaked her bloody clothes. As quickly as she could, she changed the water for the chickens and threw corn to them. Crying, she chose an outfit for João Luiz.

- My God, alone again! Am I crying for him or for me? I think I feel sorrier for myself. I'm sure João Luiz will be helped and will be fine on the spiritual plane.

She went to Danilo's house; he was waiting for her.

- I'm driving. Get in, miss; sit in the front seat. Valdete cleaned the seat, then she'll clean it again.

They went to the hospital, where she left the bag with the clothes, they would wear on João Luiz. She chose the one he liked best. Then they went to the funeral home.

- I'm going to choose this coffin: it's a child's coffin, white, and I can afford it.

Noeli tried to control herself, but tears were streaming down her face. On the way to the cemetery, she spoke:

- Mr. Danilo, the absence of people we love is very difficult. João Luiz was like an innocent child who suffered a lot. I've got used to him and I'm sure I'll miss him alone. I feel sorry for myself.

- I understand you. But answer me this: Which would be better, you alone or your friend? If he had died first, would they have let him stay in the manor? What would become of your friend? Out of love, you must think it was better that he left before you did. Don't feel sorry for yourself, don't cultivate self-pity. When we love, we really prefer to suffer in the other person's place. I think God gave you this grace, he thought you were stronger than your mother, so he took her first. Now it's your friend and you're alone again. I've been thinking about this. If I were in the afterlife and saw what my children were doing, because I'm sure they would do the same thing to Olga, I would suffer more. I'd rather suffer than see Olga suffer. I have no money for anything else. They said I did a lot of charitable work and that they needed to control me. They pay for the house, but they don't give me any money. I don't have a penny in my pocket. That's why I'm sure it was better for Olga to go to the afterlife before me.

- I'm sorry, Mr. Danilo, you don't deserve this - Noeli tried to comfort him.

- Don't you? I've been thinking about everything that's happened to me and trying to learn the lessons that need to be learned.

When they arrived at the cemetery, Father Ambrózio was there.

- Noelma, I'm so sorry! I heard what happened and I've come to help you. Where do you want to bury him?

- In my grandparents' grave, she replied.

- It's only fair, commented Father Ambrózio, he's family, the grandson of Maria and Antonieto. I'm going to pay for João Luiz's burial, he was my godson. I'll ask you to open the tomb and I'll take the opportunity to put his grandparents' bones in an office and leave a drawer vacant.

Go back to the hospital and I'll take care of everything here. Did you bring his papers?

- João Luiz didn't have any papers, he lost them. As he moved around a lot, he didn't even know where he was registered.

- I'll sort this out too, said Father Ambrózio.

- Thank you, Noeli thanked him.

- You're welcome. I loved my godson so much; I'm going to miss him.

Danilo took her to the hospital.

- God repay you, Mr. Danilo!

- I couldn't help much this time! - Danilo lamented.

- You helped me a lot! God will help you!

He went back to his house. Noeli didn't wait long at the hospital and soon saw her friend's lifeless body in the coffin. She went with him in the hearse to the cemetery. He stayed in the reception room, like his mother. Father

Ambrózio provided flowers, blessed the body, consoled Noeli and left. There were many people; some were curious, wanting to know what had happened. She repeated it many times and heard several comments: "It was imprudent!" "It had to happen!" "Nobody dies the day before! We all have our time to go!" "He's certainly in heaven!" "Couldn't he have climbed the ladder? Climbed a tree!"

Father Ambrózio scheduled the funeral for the afternoon. It was very sad for Noeli to see the tomb closed. Nalva waited for her and gave her a lift home.

When she arrived home, Noeli realized that it would rain soon. Once again, heaven is crying with me!

She changed her clothes, went to take care of the chickens and then went to make some medicine so that they wouldn't overstay their welcome. He went into the kitchen and heard Nalva calling.

- I've brought you some soup. Eat up, Sofia! You need to eat.

Noeli thanked her and drank the soup. Seeing that she was still dirty with blood, she heated some water and took a shower.

When she went into the bedroom and saw the bed that João Luiz had been using and that would now be empty, she cried a lot. She picked up her dolls and cuddled them, she hadn't picked them up for ages.

- I'm alone again!

She fell asleep, she was tired. She woke up the next morning feeling a lot of pain, her foot and ankle were very swollen. She got up and went to work.

I have to plan what I'm going to do. I can't manage on my own.

- Sofia - said a neighbor who lived across the street - Mom has a bad headache, I came to get some medicine. Will you keep making them? João Luiz will be missed! My children cried when they heard, they all loved him.

- Yes, I intend to continue making the medicines, replied Noeli.

That afternoon, she donated all her godson's clothes to the poor children. She thought about keeping something, but she preferred it to be useful, she didn't keep anything.

We keep memories in our minds, she thought determinedly.

She had little money.

It's a good thing Father Ambrózio paid for the cemetery and the flowers.

The next afternoon, she went to buy what was missing. She took home very little.

If I don't get food, I'll go hungry. That's asking for it.

A lesson for my pride.

In the evening, he read a text from the Gospel and then two pages from the notebook where he had translated texts from Kardec's book.

He saw his grandmother Maria, who told him:

- We were able to help João Luiz. He'll be fine soon. For now, he sleeps peacefully.

- Good for you! - exclaimed the lonely resident of the manor house. - I really want my godson to be well. I'll still be here alone. I have to get used to being alone!

# Chapter 9

## *IN THE HOSPITAL*

With very little to eat, on Wednesday afternoon, at the time João Luiz was picking up soup at Nalva's house, she went. She knocked on the door and the neighbor was startled to see her.

- Sofia? What are you doing here?

- I've come, Mrs. Nalva, to get the soup, she replied.

- Soup?

- Didn't João Luiz come to pick it up every Wednesday? I thought you could keep giving it to me...

- Yes, it's just that... - Nalva frowned. - In fact, João Luiz always picked her up. Today is my sister's birthday, we're going to the party, and I haven't cooked dinner. I'll give you something to eat.

- You don't have to!

Nalva went inside and came back with a paper bag.

- You can pick it up next Wednesday, said the neighbor.

- Thank you and good night!

Noeli took the package and walked away.

My God! What a situation! I thought it would be difficult to ask, but I didn't think it would be so much. Poor João Luiz, he did it so many times and didn't comment when it didn't work out. Dona Nalva was nice; if she hadn't been, I'd have heard: 'There isn't any today, come by another time'. If I still had any pride, it was suffocated. I'm a beggar!

As she passed Celeida's house, Celeida saw her and called out to her.

- Sofia! Where did you go? To Nalva's? Are you going to get some food? Nalva didn't make dinner, she's going to a party, but I did, I'll give it to you. Wait here.

He took the bowl from her hand and went into the house.

Noeli waited, trying to control herself and not cry. Soon, Celeida returned and handed her the bowl.

- Thank you, Mrs. Celeida! Thank you so much!

Noeli returned home very sad and slowly, her ankle hurting a lot. It wasn't easy to walk and she limped a lot.

Nalva gave her some bread, which was hard, but Celeida's food was tasty; she had dinner and saved the rest for lunch the next day.

She saw her mother.

- Daughter, the life we have is what we need to learn to progress. Please make an effort to get well. If you're suffering, it's because you're still proud.

She liked seeing her mother, but she couldn't console her. She felt ashamed, tired, alone and very humiliated.

The next day, Hortência, a sixteen-year-old girl, came to see her.

- Sofia, I've been helping my father work the fields since I was ten. At this time of year, there's very little work and I haven't gone with him to the fields. I really want to improve my life. I've thought about looking for a job in a family home, as a maid, but I don't know how to behave or clean a fancy house. Can't you teach me?

- I don't know much either, but what I do know, I can teach you.

Hortência went to the manor every day and helped Noeli wash her hair.

helped Noeli wash her hair.

- You won't be doing this as a maid; by helping me wash my hair, you'll learn to wash your own, and I'll make an ointment for you to apply to your face, so that you'll have beautiful skin.

With patience, the resident of the manor taught Hortência how to behave, how to eat with cutlery, how to speak properly and how to do housework.

- The houses where you'll be looking for a job are different from this manor, commented Noeli. - The important thing is to pay attention to what is explained to you, ask questions if you have any doubts and do everything as well as you can.

Hortência went to the manor every day and Noeli shared her food with her.

She went to get dinner or lunch three times a week, doing it with difficulty and feeling ashamed, sometimes turning red, but there was no other way. There were many times when she slept hungry.

One morning, when she woke up, she saw that several chickens had been stolen from her; only five remained. She cried.

If it was bad, it got worse, she lamented.

When she found out that Hortência was sleeping on the floor, she gave her the bed and mattress that were in her room.

- Thank you, Sofia! - said Hortência happily. - My two sisters and I will sleep in it. It was a wonderful present.

- Mrs. Nalva, asked Noeli when she went to fetch the soup, won't you teach Hortência to be a good maid? She can help you with the housework for a month for just lunch. By teaching her, you'll be doing a charity. Please!

Early the next morning, Hortência went to work for Nalva. And she came to the manor every Sunday to help her wash her hair.

The girl learned, stayed with Nalva for two months, then got a job and was very happy. Noeli did this with other girls: she taught them how to behave, how to eat, how to speak and how to do the basics in a house. Then Nalva stayed with them, and they learned and got jobs.

The life of the solitary resident of the manor house was routine: she fetched food, read at night, listened to the radio and experienced many needs. With two doctors and the hospital, people took less medicine and, with the theft of the chickens, the eggs dwindled and there was nothing to sell.

Even though he had difficulties, because he couldn't see very well, he read the Gospel with a magnifying glass.

And so, with many problems, Noeli turned fifty-three. A birthday she spent alone. In the evening, she saw her grandmother and mother, who came to greet her. She rejoiced and slept happily.

- Sofia! - shouted Nalva in the morning. - I've come to tell you that Mr. Danilo has died. I'm going to the wake.

If you want to go with me, come to my house in thirty minutes and I'll pick you up.

Noeli was saddened. Even though she hadn't had much contact and rarely spoke to Danilo, he was the person she could count on. She agreed to go with Nalva, went to change while crying, closed up the door and went to the neighbor's house.

She was walking with great difficulties, she felt a lot of muscle pain in her back, because she was always bent, in her ankle and in her foot.

It was sad to see her protector in the coffin. She sat in a corner of the living room and prayed for him.

- My God, may the 'thank you' and 'God repay you' I said to him be a blessing to this kind man. May you enlighten his path to the spiritual plane. May he be welcomed by the good spirits and may he be reunited with Mrs. Olga.

- Noelma - said Father Ambrózio, sitting next to her - how are you? Where was the light? When I saw you, I saw a glow around you. I think I'm old and not seeing properly. What were you doing?

- I was praying, Father Ambrózio. I was praying to God for this kind being.

- It's.... perhaps the light of prayer. Keep praying.

The priest was asked to talk to someone, and Noeli, left alone again, continued to pray for her loved ones: for Danilo, João Luiz, her mother and her grandmother. Before long, Nalva called her to leave. She thanked her neighbor and remained sad at home.

- Once again I feel sad for myself. If I need help, who will help me? I'm sure Mr. Danilo will be happy, he was a good man, he did many charities.

Two weeks after Danilo had passed away, Rosiña, his daughter, called for Noeli at the gate.

- Noeli, said Rosiña, who called her by name because she had studied with her, you know that Dad passed away and that's why we got rid of the house he lived in. That house was old and in need of renovation. We removed the furniture and now it's empty.

We decided to sell it. We saw that the electrical wiring was dangerous and asked for the power to be turned off. We don't think it's right to pay for energy without using it. I've come to warn you that at any moment you'll be without electricity. As for the water, I've decided to pay for it and you can continue to use it. However, if the new owner doesn't want to pay for the water for you, you'll be left without it.

- Water? Mr. Danilo paid for the water I use? - Noeli wondered.

- You didn't know?

- No, I only knew about the electricity.

- Dad was like that, he was very charitable! - exclaimed Rosiña.

- Thank you, Rosiña, for letting me know and for continuing to pay for the water for me.

- It's just that there are flowers in the beds that Mom used to grow. I'm coming to water them and, who knows, if the new resident likes them, he'll preserve the beds.

Rosiña left, and Noeli was heartbroken.

I won't have the light bulbs or the radio, I got used to it. It was naïve of me, I used water and I thought the town hall wouldn't charge me. I used to spend a lot of water on the vegetable garden, and Mr. Danilo paid for it. God bless him!

The next day, at dusk, the lights went out. The resident of the manor house was no longer able to read at night, she only lit one candle and carried it wherever she went. She felt very lonely. She went to bed early, woke up at dawn and was already at work at the first light of dawn.

What will I do if I run out of water? she thought worriedly.

One afternoon, she heard clapping at the gate and went to answer it. It was a girl she didn't know.

- Madam - said the girl - I need to tell you something. Noeli went to the gate and greeted her visitor.

- Good afternoon! Is that right?

- Madam, I work at the town hall. The mayor-elect is organizing several irregular properties. The tax on this house hasn't been paid for many years. It's very irregular, and the owner is reportedly missing. Isn't that, right?

- You're right, replied Noeli. - Mr. Pietro, the owner, went away many years ago and never came back.

- This property will go to the town hall because the taxes have not been paid. Can you pay off this debt?

- No, ma'am, I can't.

- On this piece of paper - the girl handed her an envelope - you are being notified that you will have to vacate the property, as it will belong to the town hall.

- What will they do with this old house? - Noeli asked.

- It will certainly be dismantled and the land sold. The area is large; a construction company will build a building. It's progress!

The girl said goodbye and Noeli, holding the envelope tightly, went into the house.

What am I going to do? I've got no power, I'm sure I'll run out of water soon, and the town hall wants to demolish the house. Will I have to live on the street?

She was called back to the gate by a neighbor from across the street.

- I've come to see if you have any medicine for a headache.

- Yes, I have some, I'll get it for you, replied the lonely woman.

With the woman were two little girls. Noeli noticed that the children were sad.

- Why are you girls so sad? - she wanted to know.

- It's because Christmas is coming and I've told them they won't get any presents. I can't afford anything, the woman replied.

Noeli took the medicine, then went to her room and got the dolls.

- You were my consolation. I like to hold them and think that they're my daughters. Now it's time for them to have other mommies.

She went back to the gate and gave the dolls away.

- They're presents!

The girls rejoiced, took the dolls and thanked her. Noeli smiled at the girls' joy.

She spent the rest of the day thinking and, no matter how hard she thought, she couldn't find a solution. She saw her grandmother, who gave her some news.

- João Luiz is very well, he's been praying a lot for you. Calm down, my granddaughter, you won't be on the street.

The next day, Sunday, Hortência went to help her wash her hair.

- Sofia, why don't you go and see the doctor at the hospital? You're very thin, pale and out of breath. If you want, I'll go with you. They're open on Sunday. I have the afternoon off. Take a shower, get dressed and let's go.

Hortência insisted, and Noeli went with her. At the hospital, the attendant said:

- Doctor Daniel will be in soon. Wait a little while.

The doctor saw her; it was the first time Noeli had been examined.

- You will be hospitalized, said the doctor.

- What? Me?

- Yes, you. You're very weak, I'm going to ask the nurse to send you to hospital, you'll be given an IV with medication.

Noeli was about to protest, but the doctor left the room.

- Stay inside, Hortência advised. - I'll stop by your house and take care of the chickens, there are only a few now.

The nurse helped her change her clothes; she took off her own, put on a hospital gown and gave her an IV. She was treated well and fed.

- It's wonderful to be here! I'm being served. Thank you, God!

The room was large, with several beds, three of which were occupied. On one bed was a girl: it was Mariana, the granddaughter of Angela, her neighbor, who was very ill.

When Angela visited her granddaughter, she went to talk to Noeli.

- Sofia, are you sick too?

- Just weak, I'll be fine soon.

- That's not what they told me. The nurse told me that you're ill and that you'll be in hospital for a few days. Mariana, my granddaughter, isn't well at all; she has cancer and today she's crying because her hair is falling out as a result of the treatment. She'll be bald!

When the visitors left, Noeli called for Mariana, who came to her bedside.

- I can't get up with the serum, said Noeli.

- Are you crying? Why are you crying? You'll be healthy again.

- Bald! Look how my hair is falling out! - Mariana put her hand to her head and it filled with hair.

- You can wear a wig - Noeli tried to console her.

- My parents are spending a lot on my treatment, and wigs are expensive. My aunt knows someone who makes wigs, but you have to have the hair.

- Yes, you do. Do you like mine? It's long and I'm sure it'll make a good wig.

- Will you give it to me? - Mariana perked up.

- It's yours!

The girl smiled, talked to her aunt and they agreed that the next day the woman who made wigs would cut Noeli's hair.

The serum ran out, another one was put in, and Noeli slept peacefully. The next day, she asked the nurse when she would be discharged, and the girl told her she would be in hospital for a few days. In the afternoon, her hair was cut.

She felt better.

- Your hair is beautiful, healthy, there aren't any white strands, it will make a nice wig! - exclaimed the woman.

- Thank you, Sofia! - thanked Mariana's mother. - Is there anything I can do for you?

- I don't need anything, thank you.

- I'd like a wig. And you, Sofia, what do you want? - Mariana asked.

- At the moment, what comes to mind is: if I die, I'd like some flowers at my wake.

They went on to talk about other things. In the evening, another doctor came to examine her.

- I'm Dr. Andrade. And who are you?

- My names are Noeli, Noeli, Sofia and Weird - she smiled.

The doctor looked at her and stood still for a moment, then spoke softly:

- I've forgotten the thermometer; I'll go and get it.

He left her side. Noeli, because she couldn't see well, didn't notice the doctor, but followed him with her gaze; he was talking to a nurse near the door.

- Is your condition really serious? - asked the doctor.

- Yes, Doctor Daniel said that her condition is serious, her heart is weak.

- I'm going to examine her and see what tests she had. I wasn't supposed to listen to them from here, thought Noeli.

- Maybe I did it to prepare myself. If I die now, nothing will change, I want to remain calm, peaceful and grateful.

The doctor and nurse left the room to talk.

- Didn't that patient have beautiful hair? - Doctor Andrade asked.

- She did until this afternoon. She donated it to Mariana to make a wig because the girl is going bald as a result of the treatment.

Doctor Andrade came into his office saying he was going to get the thermometer, but he was sorry because it was in his pocket.

Strange! I see her again after so many years, sick and uglier. She didn't recognize me! Here at the hospital, I'm called by my surname, not Antero. I don't know what for, I always remembered her and her beautiful hair. That joke always bothered me. She donated her beautiful hair! I'm going to examine her.

He returned to the infirmary and examined her; talking he learned that she was alone and very ill.

He found that her heart was weak and would stop beating at any moment.

- You should continue your treatment, advised Dr. Andrade.

- Will I be here long?

- Yes, at least ten days.

When she was alone, she thought a lot and asked a nurse to call Hortência's work and ask her to come to the hospital, as she wanted to see her.

The girl came the next day, in the afternoon.

- Hortência - said Noeli - I'm going to be in hospital for a few days. Please take the chickens and take them to your house to feed them.

- Are you sure? You like those birds so much... - Hortência said.

- I don't have any food for them and I don't want to worry about my birds getting hungry. I came to the hospital in my best clothes; if I die, I should be buried in them. If I do die, you know where I've hidden the key to the house: go in and take everything there for yourself, whatever you want, and distribute the rest to your neighbors. I only have a few things, and they belong to you. The medicines, there are some ready, they're on the shelf in the kitchen. I've marked what they're for, ask your neighbors to take them.

Hortência promised to do as she was asked. Noeli thanked her and the girl said goodbye.

Whatever's left, thought Noeli, the books and pictures on the staircase, let the town hall take them or they'll go with the house.

The next day, Doctor Andrade came to examine her. After doing so, he sat down in a chair next to the bed.

He told her that he was married, had two children, and had moved to that city in search of a quieter place to raise them.

- I'm sure they'll like it here, said Noeli.

- Are you alone? Didn't you get married? - asked the doctor.

- I didn't get married, but I loved. Love is like a flower in your life.

- Why didn't you marry him?

- He didn't even know about this love, replied the patient. - It was a joke!

If she had been seeing well, she would have seen that the doctor had gone pale. She continued:

- I've always been ugly, strange, hence the nickname, but I had, I have, feelings; this boy was the only one who paid attention to me, and I loved him.

- Have you forgiven him for the joke? - asked Dr. Andrade, trying hard not to get emotional.

- There was no reason to forgive him. It was like that...

She told us about the meeting, that she overheard the boys talking in the area, and it was over:

- They were inconsequential young people, they didn't mean any harm, and it was good, I had love. I loved him. I wish him happiness!

The nurse called for the doctor.

- I'll be back later. Take care, said Dr. Andrade.

Why did I feel like telling him that story? thought Noeli, asking herself. It's in the past. Only my mother knew about it. I hope this doctor doesn't tell anyone. Dr. Andrade paid attention to me, he kept asking, and I answered. That's why I told him, because of the attention he gave me. I'd better forget this story for good. Even if he asks, I won't talk about this love anymore. This feeling took up a space in my heart that wasn't divided. I'm glad it was only a small piece. Because the love that occupied the larger space was shared many, many times. And this has only done me good.

Doctor Andrade left Noeli's side and went to see other patients. When he was alone, he thought:

- God forgive me! I never thought that a bet, a joke, could have made someone suffer. She told me a secret, and I'm not going to tell anyone that the stranger loved, had a love. I'm glad Noeli didn't recognize me. She loved Antero, and today I'm Doctor Andrade. From what I've heard, she's suffered a lot. I'm going to treat her well, she deserves it.

Upset by the youthful prank, because it had never crossed his mind that, for a simple encounter, she could have fallen in love and suffered, he felt remorse. Twice a day, he went to the ward where Noeli was and talked to her, but he never touched on the past again. The patient got worse and could no longer get out of bed.

Mariana was completely bald, but the wig was ready, and she felt good, because the wig was so beautiful.

- What do you do when someone you can't afford dies? How do you bury them? - Noeli asked a nurse.

- We notify the hospital's social services, and they do the burial, she replied.

Father Ambrózio came to visit her and explained:

- I come to the hospital every week to visit the sick; each time I come; I go to a ward.

- How nice of you to come! - exclaimed Noeli.

- I wanted to talk to you.

- Do you want to go to confession?

- No. I think I'm going to die. That doesn't scare me. I've lived this life without doing anything bad, I've tried to be honest and I've prayed a lot. I'd like to ask you to do me a favor: bury me or see if the social services will do it. I would like to be buried in my grandparents' grave. Will you do this for me?

- If I don't die first, I will. You're being well looked after and you'll get better and go home soon.

-Home? I don't think I have a home anymore. Mr. Danilo, my kind ex-neighbor, used to pay for the electricity and water for me; when he died, his children disconnected the power, and Hortência told me that there's no water in the manor house, so it must have been disconnected too. The town hall is expropriating the house because the tax hasn't been paid for many years. If it does get better, I'd like you to help me get to the nursing home in the next town.

- What about your medicines? - the priest wanted to know.

- As long as I could, I made them. You can't make them without water, the plants have to be watered.

- I hope you get better. Noelma, when you're well, I'll get you a place in the asylum.

- What if I die? - Noeli asked.

- I'll give you my blessings and do as you ask

- Thank you very much!

- Do you believe that "thank you" and "God repay you" are blessings? - asked the priest.

- Yes, I do.

- I'll try to be more charitable to receive these blessings. Stay with God! - Father Ambrózio said goodbye.

Doctor Andrade, whenever he passed by the ward, greeted her and asked how she was.

Noeli didn't complain. As she rested, the pain eased, her ankle hurt less, she wasn't hungry anymore, but she was panting and breathing hard.

- I'm fine, thank you! - she always replied.

Antero de Andrade no longer spoke to her about private matters. He was kind to all the sick people, but more so to her.

That afternoon, he took a closer look at her.

She's very thin, she has very few teeth, and they're damaged; with her hair cut short, she looks old and like a child at the same time. She's dying, medicine can't help her. From what I've been told, her being here is the return of all the good she's done. She won't die alone and she has the comfort of being supported.

- Noeli, if you want anything, just ask. Would you like something different? - asked Dr. Andrade, eager to do something for the sick woman.

- No, sir, I don't need anything. I'm being treated very well. May God protect you and may you continue to be a kind and humane doctor.

The doctor's eyes filled with tears; at that moment, he felt like telling her who he was, but he didn't. She would have been embarrassed, he said.

- She'd be embarrassed; she certainly wouldn't want to be in front of her past love like she is now.

It was eight days since she had been in hospital; that morning, she had breakfast and then settled into bed. She remembered the past with nostalgia. Scenes from her childhood came to mind, playing with her grandparents. She saw when Pietro said goodbye and how he looked at her. She remembered many events with her mother. Then the wounded man in the area and João Luiz. She moved her feet, looked at them and saw that they were perfect. She smiled. She ran her hand over her head and felt her hair: it was loose, silky and clean. He smiled again. She felt good, very good, and slept peacefully.

# Chapter 10

## *CHANGE*

- Good morning, Sofia! - greeted a nurse. - How did you spend the night? Have you had your breakfast? Sofia! Oh my God!

The nurse took Noeli's hand and noticed that it was cold, she couldn't feel a pulse. She quickly went in search of the doctor, found Dr. Daniel, and the two of them approached the bed where Noeli lay. The doctor listened to her.

- She was dead! It was expected. She died peacefully. Please take action, the doctor asked the nurse.

Quietly, so as not to frighten the other patients, the two of them left the room. The arrangements were made: they took Noeli's lifeless body out of the room, took it to the proper place, put her clothes on, arranged for a simple coffin, notified the priest and some neighbors and, in a mortuary urn, she was taken to the cemetery. Word spread that Noeli had given her beautiful hair and asked for flowers in return. The neighbors went to the wake and brought flowers. Even the residents across the street came, took the flowers they had at home and picked up the ones from the manor house.

Doctor Andrade heard about Noeli's death as soon as he arrived at the hospital.

- She believed that life goes on. May this continuity be one of great peace for her, said the doctor.

- Mrs. Rosely, you're finishing your shift, aren't you? - asked Dr. Andrade. - Could you do me a favor? Buy me a bouquet of roses and take them to the wake. I won't be able to leave the hospital until the evening, I have a delivery and surgery. I want to give flowers to Noeli.

- You got attached to her, you talked to her. I'll buy the flowers for you and take them to the cemetery.

- Thank you!

Antero de Andrade missed talking to Noeli and was saddened by her death. He was distracted by work and had plenty to do that day.

Father Ambrózio organized everything and the wake was decorated with flowers.

- Sofia seemed to be smiling!

- She died as quietly as she ever lived!

- She wanted some flowers and she got plenty!

- It's such a beautiful day! Sofia died on a beautiful day!

- Her expression is calm! She's smiling! There were many comments, but there was no crying.

Father Ambrózio gave the blessing and the funeral took place in the afternoon. After three days of rain, it was a beautiful day.

Hortência and her neighbors went to the manor house and took everything they could use: furniture, kitchen utensils, the bed and the few vegetables from the garden.

- All that will be left are these ugly paintings and the books, said Hortência. - Now the town hall can dismantle this house.

Hortência locked the house and left the key where Noeli had hidden it.

- We've run out of medicine! - exclaimed one of her neighbors.

Some of those poor women, who had been receiving help for years for any pain, felt sorry for themselves; they would be without the Stranger's medicines.

Noeli woke up and opened her eyes slowly.

- I dreamt of flowers, lots of flowers! - she said softly.

She looked to the side and saw her hair. She wiggled her toes and pulled back the sheet.

- I'm still dreaming! I've never dreamt like this.

- Good morning! How are you feeling, Noeli? - a girl dressed in white greeted her.

- I'm fine, thank you! Did I wake up? I'm feeling a bit... different - replied Noeli, preferring not to say "strange".

- You slept for three days. You woke up and you're fine, right?

- I slept, I woke up and I'm still dreaming?

- Why do you think you're dreaming? - asked the girl.

- My hair, I've cut it - Noeli ran her hand through her hair - my feet are the same, and I don't feel short of breath. I think I can get up and jump.

- Then do it. Get up and jump.

Noeli smiled, got up from the bed easily and realized that she was wearing a very nice, clean nightgown. She looked down at her feet, they were really healthy; her legs were the same size; she was slender; and she could see perfectly. She jumped about three times. She laughed.

- Let's hope it takes her a while to wake up! - she exclaimed.

- Noeli - said the girl - I'm glad you're feeling well, but you're not sleeping.

- No? - asked Noeli, stopping jumping.

- What's going on?

- There are people outside wanting to see you, to welcome you. I'll ask them to come in.

Noeli, surprised, saw her grandmother and mother.

- What a perfect dream! Oh, my God! Grandma! Mom! She hugged them and received lots of kisses.

- Mom, I don't want to wake up!

- You're awake, my dear, said Violeta. – You have disincarnated.

- I don't mind waking up tired, not after this dream!

- My dear, said Maria, pay attention, you're not asleep or dreaming.

- Are you ladies all right? - asked Noeli, not paying attention to what she was being told.

- Now I'm going to lie down again, to sleep and wake up. I love you both!

He lay down on the bed and settled in. Maria and Violeta smiled. Noeli closed her eyes and felt asleep.

She woke up hours later. She opened her eyes and looked at where she was.

- I feel awake and in the place of my dream. My hair and feet are healthy, I met Grandma and Mom and this time it was different, they were like me or... me like them. Could it be that I'm in the afterlife?

He got up slowly and walked around the room.

I walk easily, I breathe naturally, I don't feel any pain. Could I be disincarnated?

- Good afternoon! How...

- Disincarnated? - Noeli interrupted the girl who had just come in.

- Yes, my dear, you've changed planes.

- On the physical plane, I didn't move house, I lived all my life in the manor house. Now I've changed...

- You've made a great and good change. You're among friends.

Soon your grandmother and mother will come to see you.

Noeli walked around the room, she was happy to walk and her ankle didn't hurt. Soon Maria and Violeta entered the room.

- Grandma, Mom, I understand, my physical body has died and I'm in the afterlife.

- Yes, my granddaughter, said Maria, you've made a change, you're among us now.

- I want to know many things, said Noeli. - And Grandpa Nieto?

- Antonieto - replied Maria - he reincarnated a while ago, he's fine.

- And my uncles? Your sons?

- They both disincarnated at a young age and are currently in their fleshly bodies. I visit them whenever I can.

- Mom, who is my father? Do you know?

- Pietro, Violeta answered quietly. - It was Mr. Pietro who raped me. He was obsessed, he was disturbed, but he had no justification for his evil act. He knew, as did Mrs. Eleodora. Pietro went to India, entered a monastery, got rid of the obsession, contracted a fever and disincarnated. He is currently reincarnated in India.

- Why do I have my hair? Why am I healthy? - asked the newly disincarnated woman.

- Your deficiencies, Maria replied, were due to your fleshly body. Your spirit became healthy through the resignation with which you suffered. You gave away your favorite dolls and even let go of your hair, which is so beautiful. She did a good deed by giving them away. They are yours. Your perispirit is healthy and harmonious; it's beautiful. Your teeth are healthy, your color is good and your hair is long.

- Grandma - Noeli wanted to know - was Antônio, who disincarnated in the area, Mr. Thomas in his last incarnation?

- You're very curious! Yes, my granddaughter, Antônio was Thomas. We were able to help him and he has been trying hard to learn here on the spiritual plane and to be useful.

- Could I read Allan Kardec's books? - asked Noeli.

- Not just read them, but join a study group, replied Maria. - Thinking that you would want that, I decided to take you later to the group that is studying *The Mediums' Book*. You'll like it.

- You're leaving the hospital, said Violeta, you're only in this ward to recover. You'll go to our house.

The newly disincarnated woman got excited, she didn't know whether to laugh or cry with emotion, it was such a joy to be living with her grandmother and mother again; she preferred to laugh and she did, she changed and put on a nice outfit.

- This outfit is my present! - Maria exclaimed.

- It's beautiful!

They left the hospital, crossed the street and walked a few blocks. Noeli didn't get tired of walking, she looked at everything with delight, the streets were tree-lined and very clean. They reached the house where Maria and Violeta lived.

- This house is also yours. Let's see your room

- Maria took her by the hand.

Noeli excitedly visited the house and found it beautiful.

- How beautiful the flowers are here! - she exclaimed.

After seeing everything, she met the other residents, had a soup which she found very tasty and went to bed.

The next day, he walked around the house and the garden. He still slept a lot, eight hours; his grandmother or mother kept him company. Three days passed. Maria took her to see the colony.

- I've never seen such a beautiful city. Everything so clean...

- In the evening, said Maria, I'm going to take you to the course. A group of thirty people are studying The Mediums' Book.

- I'm looking forward to it.

Maria, Violeta and Noeli went to the school, where the group was meeting in a room. Everyone was holding a book. Noeli was given a copy. The instructor asked them to open to chapter XIII, "Psychography". Sonia, a participant, read the first paragraph and commented. Anyone who wanted to speak raised their hand and could ask questions.

In this way, several paragraphs were read and commented on.

Noeli paid attention and really enjoyed the lesson.

- I'm going to read this book and underline anything I don't understand and then ask the instructor. It's a pity I didn't start with the group. That's okay: when they start another one, I'll do it again. I'm going to love this study. Grandma, was I really Noellii?

- Yes, my dear. We reincarnate many times.

We live sometimes on the spiritual plane and sometimes on the physical one.

- I made a lot of mistakes as the lady of the manor!

Noeli sighed and memories came back to her. She saw herself as a little girl, poor, and her mother, a prostitute. She traveled with her aunt, who was stern and bad-tempered. She went to a distant country with different customs. Her aunt arranged a marriage which, in her opinion, was advantageous. Noeli never loved Thomas or her daughter. To keep herself entertained, she took lovers and ended up having abortions.

- Maria explained that mistakes usually give us some form of pleasure. It's the wide door. However, mistakes, by law, have returns that lead us to suffer. Through pain comes regret and the desire to get it right. Making mistakes is easy, but the consequences are not. When we reincarnate, we usually think about mastering this conditioning, not making any more mistakes, but for many of us, overcoming this test is difficult. We are drawn to return, on the physical plane, to affections or, unfortunately, to attach ourselves through bad feelings to those we don't like. We may also return to places, as you did.

- Grandma, Mom, have we been together in other lives?

We love each other so much...

- Violeta and I, yes, Maria replied, but with you, we only met in the manor house, we had very little contact. In fact, we love each other very much. That's the important thing, to learn to love everyone.

- My disincarnating as a Noeli was very different from my last one. I'm enjoying being here so much... Even more so because I'm not worried about anyone or anything.

- I worried a lot about you, said Violeta.

- Being here and thinking about you there made me sad. However, I realized that our separation was necessary and temporary.

- How bad it is to disincarnate disharmonized... I'm remembering that I suffered a lot when I left my physical body in my incarnation as the lady of the manor.

- Unfortunately, you transmitted this maladaptation to the physical body when you reincarnated, Maria explained.

- I think I was afraid of being beautiful! - Noeli exclaimed. - If I had been beautiful, would I have lived as I did? Being beautiful could have prevented me from doing what I did. Is physical beauty a proof?

- It could be, replied Maria. - I didn't worry about this aspect. I was beautiful when I was incarnate and it made no difference to me. If you think that being beautiful is difficult, beauty can be a test for you.

- I think, my dear, that you won't have any trouble overcoming this test, if you think you have to go through it. But at the moment, there's a lot to do and learn here. You'll have to spend a few years on the spiritual plane before you can think about reincarnating.

- I feel that I will have to go through this test and I feel like testing myself.

- It can be postponed, said Maria.

Noeli noticed that everyone was working there and, a few days later, she asked her grandmother.

- What do you do, Grandma?

- I work with the incarnate, helping them. I used to help you make medicines. My granddaughter, when I was incarnate, I tried to be useful by making medicines. I saw the grace within me. We must all enhance the grace we have received.

First, see this grace, feel it, enhance it and, with it, do what we have to do, help others with love. I try to help sick people. Everything is energy, and illness is energy too. There are people who, for many reasons, have learned to help other people heal, whether through prayers, the laying on of hands or other ways, because they know how to use the power of love to illuminate other people's illnesses. They donate salutary energies that weaken and even exterminate the sick energy. When you made your remedies, you wanted to heal the pain of others and you succeeded. I hope, Noeli, that you, now disincarnate, will come and learn from me and, together, we'll continue to ease the pain.

- Yes, Grandma, I want to help you. I feel good, I see everyone working and I want to learn. And Mom, what are you doing?

- Violeta is learning, she goes to school, she has learned to read and write and also to be useful. She works in a ward at the hospital.

- Patients here? - Noeli asked in amazement.

- To disincarnate and feel healthy, to have a healthy perispirit, you need to be spiritually well. To have suffered resignedly, like you, for the illness to remain only in the physical body.

Noeli had been in the colony for nine days. In the afternoon, she picked up a book to read.

I want to learn to work, to be useful, and reading is a way of learning. Has João Luiz read The Mediums' Book? Where is he that I haven't seen him yet? Why hasn't he come to visit me?

He tried to concentrate on his reading, but he kept thinking about his friend/son. Early the next morning, when he saw his grandmother, he wanted to know about his friends.

- Grandma, I'd like to know about Mr. Danilo and Mrs. Olga.

- Olga was helped as soon as she passed away. The attitude of her husband, her companion of many years, helped her.

- Danilo wanted his wife to be well and not to worry about him and the children. Olga stayed with us and tried to stay well, just as her husband wanted. And there were many grateful people who wanted to help Danilo. He disincarnated among spiritual friends, was helped and reunited with Olga. They are together and doing well, studying and learning to live disincarnate in order to be useful. As soon as possible, I'll take you to visit them.

- I'd like to see them again and thank them. Grandma, what about João Luiz? Why haven't I seen him yet? Did he turn out like me? Healthy and with all his teeth? Is he tall?

- João Luiz was with us, but he's not here anymore.

- What happened? - Noeli asked.

- He left without permission and went to the crust, near the incarnates.

- How is that possible?

- We have our free will, replied Maria.

- When a person disincarnates, they receive help because they deserve it and can be assisted in many places, but whether they stay in these shelters depends on whether they want to or not. Some people, although they like it, don't stay.

- What happens then?

- Not being prepared to be around incarnate people, they usually get upset and even fall ill; they complicate their lives and the lives of those they stay close to.

- But where did João Luiz go? He didn't go to the manor; I didn't see him.

- To the circus? Did he want revenge for his mistreatment?

- No - Maria clarified - he didn't go to the circus where he worked. His forgiveness was sincere: if he had wanted revenge, he wouldn't have been brought to this colony. Hatred and a desire for revenge are incompatible feelings for receiving help.

- Grandma, please explain to me what happened to my godson, asked the newly disincarnated woman.

- We helped João Luiz to hospital. Because he was injured, you and Danilo took him to the hospital. We disconnected his spirit from dead matter and brought him with us. He was happy to be feeling well. He came here, to this home of ours. We helped him change his appearance. His disability was physical. He grew taller, his face softened. He was fine. He took to reading Allan Kardec's books. Then his godson made a request: he wanted to visit Gracia.

- His love! - Noeli clarified. - So, Grandma, was he able to see her again?

- He had permission; an instructor would accompany him on this visit. Gracia was in a distant city, in another country, in a circus. João Luiz was excited; he couldn't wait to go. However, he returned from the visit very sad and told Violeta and me that he had found Gracia leading a very difficult life. She had three children, no longer worked as a performer, but at the box office, and her children were rebellious and didn't respect her. Her husband was a partner in the circus, had a young mistress and humiliated Gracia. She was ill and didn't receive proper treatment. He talked about her for a couple of days, and also told her that the instructor who had accompanied him had forced him to return. One morning, as he was leaving for work, he said to me: Grandma Maria, when you can, tell Noeli that I'm fine. Thank you for everything. When she returned in the afternoon, Violeta told me that João Luiz had left. He'd left a note thanking me and telling me he was going away. I went after him and found him near Gracia. I tried to convince him to come back; I explained that without preparation and permission, he would soon get upset and that nobody helps without knowing. I gave the example that someone who doesn't know how to sew, no matter how much they want to, won't make a dress. You have to know how to sew. His godson listened quietly and then said to me: "I'm going to stay here and whatever God wants". I went back to the colony alone, and he stayed.

- Does this happen a lot? - Noeli wanted to know. - That the disincarnate don't stay here and come back to the incarnate? It's so beautiful here, so harmonious... How can someone want to leave this place?

- There are many reasons, Maria replied. - Many people feel attached to what they thought was theirs, material things. Mistakenly, they felt that they possessed rather than temporarily administered. Others feel attached to those they love. And others, for specific reasons, like João Luiz, want to stay close to the people they love.

- Aren't there also those who want revenge? - Noeli asked.

- Yes, but they can't even be helped. I told you about those who are helped and don't stay, they go back to the places where their affections or objects are. My granddaughter, in order to be helped and to be in a colony or aid station, you have to deserve it. When they disincarnate, many reckless people can't be helped because they don't fit in with these places of love. There are many dwellings in the father's house, many places where a disincarnate person can be. We are drawn to similar places. A person who has not acted correctly, who has done wrong, cannot be here; nor can those who have not forgiven, because those who do not forgive are not forgiven.

- I remember some things from my previous reincarnation, but my change of plane was very different from the last one. I did bad things; I wasn't forgiven by some people. I had to suffer to ask for forgiveness.

- Thank God this one was different! This is a sign that you have suffered, learned, made an effort and improved yourself.

- I wanted to help my godson. Please, Grandma, take me to him, maybe I can convince him to come back.

- I'll ask permission.

Maria left and returned soon after.

- I can accompany you to visit João Luiz. We'll go by airbus; a vehicle we use on the spiritual plane to get around. We could fly, but I'd rather use this vehicle so that you can meet him. Let's go?

- Thank you, Grandma, I really want to talk to my godson.

Noeli marveled at the journey. Twelve residents of the colony went to the crust.

- We're going to stay for five hours, said Maria.

- If I can convince him, that's enough time. The vehicle stopped at a place.

- This is an aid station, Maria continued. - Now we're going to fly. Take my hand. Don't be afraid.

- I'm not afraid, Grandma, I trust you. I'm not scared, but amazed. Everything is fantastic! Exciting!

Holding her grandmother's hand tightly, the two of them moved around; Noeli felt as if she were flying. Soon they saw a circus. The large, colorful canvas occupied a space in a medium-sized town. There was a lot of movement in the place, the artists were rehearsing. Soon the two saw him.

He was standing next to a woman they recognized as Gracia. They were both sad. Noeli observed her friend. João Luiz looked very different, he must have been one meter and forty centimeters taller than when he was incarnate and was ninety centimeters tall; his features had changed.

- João Luiz - Maria explained - is becoming disabled again, because he's getting upset. It was expected. Normally, disincarnate people who leave without permission and those who stay wandering get upset and think they are still incarnate. Go and talk to him, I'll be around but your godson won't see me, it's better that way. I'll help you.

As they approached, the two noticed the incarnate woman. Gracia was apprehensive, worried, she was certainly going through difficulties. She had beautiful expressions, but she was aged and overweight.

- João Luiz! - Noeli called out. - How are you, friend? He looked at her, observing her, then asked:

- Do I know you?

Violeta's daughter understood that he hadn't recognized her because he was getting upset, as Maria had explained.

- Don't you remember me? I'm Noeli, your godmother and friend.

- Noeli, Noeli... I don't know. Where do I know you from?

- Can I sit next to you? - Noeli sat down next to him. - Don't you remember the manor, the garden, the medicines?

- The manor? The big house of my uncle Thomas and his fiery wife? My memories are confused. I see the manor house in ruins and I remember the medicines... I used to help someone make them. But who are you? Noeli?

Maria, who was standing next to her granddaughter, spoke softly:

- Don't talk about the past. Make him remember only the last incarnation, of you both in the house.

- João Luiz, I'm Noeli, your godmother. You lived with me in the big house where we made medicines for sick people.

- I liked making medicines. Couldn't you help me make one for sadness? Gracia is so sad! Her husband has a mistress, a young artist. Her three children are in trouble, and she's sick and tired.

- I'll make one for her, said Noeli. - Don't you remember me?

- I remember your hair, it's beautiful. You look different.

- You look different too! - exclaimed Noeli.

- Me? I don't know!

- João Luiz, pay attention. Remember! - she asked.

Noeli saw Maria give her godson a pass. He looked at her and suddenly recognized her and exclaimed happily:

- Noeli! Sofia! Stranger! Godmother! You're here!

- I'm gone, my godson. My body died like yours. I was supported and worried about you, who left the shelter without permission.

- Gracia is going through difficulties and I've come to help her.

- Only those who know help. If you don't know, you could get in her way.

- I don't want to get in your way! Tell me: How did you die? How are you?

- My heart stopped, replied Noeli. - I was in hospital.

- I was rescued and I'm with my mom and grandma. I really enjoyed the camp and I'm happy. I wanted to see you again and they told me that you left the colony to be with Gracia. João Luiz, as much as you love her, you mustn't interfere in her life. We all have our lessons to learn. By staying by her side without any knowledge, you could obsess her, drain her energy and harm her.

- Remember Allan Kardec's *The Mediums' Book*? Do you want to become an obsessed?

- No way! Do you believe, Godmother, that I can harm you?

- Yes, I'm sure. In order to stop feeding yourself, to stop feeling hungry, you need to know how to do it - Noeli repeated what Maria was telling her. - So now, in order to feel fed, you're draining Gracia's energy, making her condition worse. You've suffered and you know that I've suffered too. We all go through difficulties. Don't try to teach your loved one a lesson, it won't work, because it's she who needs to go through these difficulties. You mustn't stay close to her, because if you don't know how to help, you'll get in the way. Come back with me, please.

- I think you're right. I'm getting smaller and smaller, and my face is changing too. Will I be a dwarf again?

- We can change. The body we use now, the perispirit, is changeable. Your disability and mine were of the physical body. Look at my feet, they're healthy. However, if you get upset, you may feel your body's deficiency again and you may look like a dwarf again. I've come for you. Come back with me, my godson! Let's study Allan Kardec's books together. We want this so much! When you're ready, if you wish, you can ask me to come and help you. Then it will be different, you will really help.

- I think you're right - João Luiz sighed. - Gracia has been complaining that she's getting weaker and sadder. I'll go with you.

Maria made herself visible to him.

- Grandma Maria! Help Gracia for me, please! - pleaded João Luiz, hugging her.

- I'll help her!

Maria gave Gracia passes, and she sighed with relief and exclaimed softly:

- Thank God I'm feeling better! I'm going to work!

She got up and went elsewhere. João Luiz looked at her sadly.

- I don't want to hurt you, Godmother. I love you!

- I know you do!

- If it's for your peace of mind, João Luiz, said Maria, I'll take you to the colony, then I'll come back and try to help you.

- Thank you, Grandma Maria, thank you very much!

Maria hugged them and they went to the place where they would wait for the airbus to return to the colony.

When they arrived, godmother and godson sat down in a corner and talked, one telling the other how they felt about being disincarnated.

- I told João Luiz, felt a strong pain in my chest when I was wounded. I thought I had fainted, but I disincarnated. I soon suspected that I had changed planes. Grandma Maria and Aunt Violeta helped me and, feeling well, my appearance changed, I became tall and handsome. I wanted to see Gracia again. After seeing her, I wanted to be with her and I sneaked out of the colony. Can't I really be with her?

- No, my friend, not for now, replied Noeli.

- I'm feeling sleepy. I'm going to take a nap. - João Luiz put his head on his godmother's shoulder and fell asleep.

- I put him to sleep, said Maria, so that he wouldn't feel the need to go back to the circus, to Gracia. Let's take him asleep.

Maria put him on a stretcher. At the appointed time, the vehicle arrived, they settled in and returned to the colony.

# Chapter 11
## *THE COLONY*

João Luiz woke up feeling upbeat, and Noeli offered to help him, to stay with him and encourage him to stay in the colony. They studied, read together and strolled around the city on the spiritual plane. They both loved the place.

- What I admire here is that everyone is kind or is trying hard to be, said João Luiz.

- What I admire most is the cleanliness. Nobody gets dirty or throws anything on the ground, they look after everything as if it were their own. Everyone grows flowers, trees and respects nature.

- In the future, the colonies will be imitated by incarnates, commented João Luiz.

- When that happens, the cities on the physical plane will be beautiful, ideal homes.

She tried in every way to distract her friend, she didn't want him to leave again, because, as Maria had told her, they would no longer be allowed to pick him up. If he went out hiding, he would only be rescued again if he asked for it, if he begged for it, and he would probably go somewhere else, to an aid station.

The two of them talked a lot.

- Have you ever noticed, commented João Luiz, that, depending on the interests of those who are here, there is an activity that catches their attention the most? You admire plants. Leonice, who lives with us, the schools; she enthusiastically talks about the teachings that can be obtained on the spiritual plane. Grandma Maria is enthusiastic about the work you can do with incarnates. Soledade talks enthusiastically about how the colony is run. Maria das Dores, in her spare time, goes to the library and always has a book in her hand. I've seen young people enthusiastic about the gadgets available in this town. Sandro likes electricity and says he's going to ask to work in this area to learn; he intends to dedicate himself to this task when he's reincarnated.

Yesterday I saw a group studying and researching remedies for diseases.

- That's wonderful! - exclaimed Noeli. - I think that if the colonies were described by several residents, each one would highlight the part that interests them most. And you, my friend, what do you like best?

- At the moment, I have one goal: to learn in order to work with incarnates.

- I'm thinking of studying everything about agronomy later, if that's possible. I really want to be able to value the food that the earth produces in my next incarnation. I could have done this and I didn't. I also like music and I'm thinking of learning to play an instrument. Did you know, godmother, that I was called João Luiz in my previous incarnation? Was it a coincidence that you gave me this name or were you instructed?

- It was the first name that came to mind that day, she replied.

- When I stopped on the road, I went to the old manor house as if drawn by a magnet. I was hoping to find the luxury of yesteryear. Everything does pass. You helped me a lot by letting me stay there, it was my home. Like João Luiz, I used to go to the manor as a visitor. Do you remember me?

- Before you arrived at the manor, replied Noeli, I had a vision of myself as Noeli and João Luiz, and I saw the two of them arguing on the stairs.

- During the argument, I fell and was disincarnated. What a change of plan! I stayed in the dead body, not wanting to leave it until burial time; then I obsessed Noeli with great anger, until my enemies, the enemies I had made, took me to the threshold. I suffered, I repented, I asked for help, I was helped and soon after I reincarnated.

- Did you remember everything that happened to you in your past existence? - Noeli wanted to know.

- The obsessor who tormented me when I was in the circus always told me about what he had done. I was born into a financially well-off family; my father was a farmer who owned a lot of land. I was handsome, I abused everything, I spent a lot of money, so much so that I wanted to marry Eleodora to keep what she had inherited. I had no qualms about being my uncle's wife's mistress. In fact, I did everything I could think of: I didn't respect anyone, raped, abused, used my social status, money and beauty to dominate and make people unhappy.

- Behind one of the paintings in the room, one of the ones you sold, I found a letter that had belonged to Mr. Thomas and that said you might be his son.

- I knew that, said João Luiz. - My mother had told me and said it might be useful, but she told me it wasn't true. It's not a justification, but my family wasn't honest back then. It was an existence that I remember with great sadness. In the manor house, I also had flashes of memories of the past, of the proud João Luiz. But I didn't say anything for fear of your reaction, that you would send me away.

- I also didn't say much about my memories for the same reason: I was afraid you wouldn't forgive me, that you'd want to take revenge, that you'd be hurt by me. In the past, I didn't want you to fall down the stairs and disincarnate; in the present, I didn't want you to leave. That's why I didn't tell you.

- How nice! - he exclaimed. - We took the opportunity, reconciled and learned to love each other like brothers. I'm grateful to God for that. We should have talked about our memories, exchanged information.

- Talk about the past? I think we did the right thing. The past can't be changed and it's the present that's important.

- Our experience in the manor is already in the past!

- The recent past, agreed Noeli. - Maybe this one should be discussed, but the one from the incarnation before this one, with so many mistakes, is better left in the past.

- If we remember, it's because there are reasons. It was a learning opportunity. Mistakes cause the wrong to become disharmonized and, to achieve harmony, it's either through love, by doing good, or through pain. We have suffered, but we have also done good, especially you. This incarnation of ours has been one of great learning.

- We learned why we suffered. Many suffer without knowing it. The important thing is not to rebel and to learn. It's the present that's important to me. My present is one of joy and learning.

- I want to learn a lot, decided João Luiz. - I talked to the instructor of the course studying Allan Kardec's books and he told me that we can choose what we work on and where. I've already made my choice. As soon as possible, I'm going to join a group of rescuers who work to help incarnate people. I'm going to be part of a team at an aid station in the country where Gracia's circus is located. At this aid station, I'll work certain hours a day, and I'll have time to visit you and help you when necessary.

- You remember a lot about your past. Gracia is certainly a friend, a dear spirit. Have you ever lived together? - Noeli wanted to know.

- I remember very little about my other incarnations. It's better this way. I wasn't a saint in any of them. Gracia and I have been together, incarnate and discarnate. I love her and I was loved, but I feel we didn't do the right thing. When I was João Luiz and made a lot of mistakes, we didn't meet. I don't know if Gracia still loves me. She doesn't remember the past. Like most people, she has completely forgotten her other incarnations and perhaps she doesn't even remember her disincarnated self. Many memories can be disturbing. When I was by her side last month, I tried to make her remember me at the circus; she didn't, at least I didn't feel it. I don't know how to hear thoughts yet, but I'll learn.

They no longer talked about the past; they had their memories. They made mistakes, they harmonized through the pain and the good they had done. Noeli concluded that the memories she had when she was incarnate had been a blessing and had made her understand that everything, she had been through was a learning experience. She decided not to think about the past anymore, because it is in the present moment that we decide our future. She planned to be useful in the future and to learn a lot.

João Luiz began to sleep very little.

- Godmother, you're a sleeper!

- I like to sleep - she argued.

- Let's go to the volitation course, João Luiz invited her, then to the nutrition course, and after that I'm going to learn the language of the country where I plan to work. I do the courses on Kardec's books and I love studying them. I can't wait to start the one that teaches me how to work with incarnates. Now I'm waiting for Grandma Maria, she's gone to visit Gracia and she'll let me know.

João Luiz was restless and, as soon as he saw Maria, he asked:

- How is Gracia?

- I removed the two obsessors who were harming her husband. Without these negative energies, he is calmer and has treated her well. Her children are also calmer and Gracia's health has improved.

- Thanks be to God! Thank you, Grandma Maria! - thanked João Luiz.

With his goal set, João Luiz learned to fly much earlier than Noeli; enthusiastically, he did exercises at home to learn how to nourish himself, read a lot, learned the language he wanted and went on a course on how to help incarnates. Maria took him to visit Gracia; this time he came back happy and commented to his godmother.

- You really help the discarnate who knows. Grandma Maria really helped Gracia: she's healthier, she doesn't fight anymore, her children's rebelliousness has improved and she doesn't mind her husband's betrayal, as she's starting to get sick of his mistress.

- Do you really want to work in this aid station just to see Gracia? - Noeli wanted to know.

- When I came back here and was brought here by you, I thought that; then, as I studied, I realized that everything we do has to be done with love. It will be a great experience to work with an aid team. I also want to improve myself, to direct my feelings towards the good, I will learn to love Gracia as a sister.

Noeli studied hard and spent four hours a day with her mother in the wards of the colony hospital. At first, she even cried, feeling sorry for the patients. Then she realized that pity without action is useless. So, she prayed before and after and, with affection, helped Violeta to look after those who returned to the spiritual plane sick in the soul. Many there felt the pain of remorse. She cleaned them up, gave them water, food and words of comfort and love.

While João Luiz was enthusiastic, Noeli began to worry and ended up complaining to her grandmother.

- I really like this place. The colony is just lovely. Everyone here is committed to helping teach and I've already made a lot of friends. Although everything is perfect for me, I'm feeling restless. I feel like I'm being asked for help. At the hospital I try to do everything right. They don't ask me for anything there, but they ask Mom, who has been working there for a long time. Am I confusing myself? Why am I feeling this way?

- Noeli, you know that my task is to help people who are in the crust. When I was incarnate, I made the remedies out of a desire to heal pain. Nenvis, a disincarnated friend of mine, who was a doctor when he put on his physical body, used to guide me; after I moved to the afterlife, we started working together.

- Grandma - Noeli interrupted her - when I heard you talking about doctors, I remembered Dr. Andrade. He was very kind to me in hospital.

- Think of him, of Doctor Andrade, Maria asked.

- It came to my mind that he asked a nurse to buy flowers, red roses, and take them to my wake. How delicate! I don't understand. Why did he do that?

- You wanted flowers at your wake...

- I didn't want anything, she interrupted again. - I just thought a wake without flowers was sad.

- When you gave your hair to Mariana to make a wig, she asked for flowers.

- What did I do? I didn't really want them. Poor flowers that decorate wakes. Flowers should decorate life.

- Remember that life is one. Think, my granddaughter, of Dr. Andrade, Maria asked.

- I am thinking. I see him clearly now.

- Don't you recognize him? - asked her grandmother.

- He looks like someone. Who does he look like? Tell me, Grandma.

- This doctor is called Antero de Andrade.

- He's Antero? - Noeli was surprised. - The Antero I loved? Incredible! Grandma, I told him about my love. Shame on you!

- No shame at all! - Maria exclaimed. - She was by his side that day. Antero recognized her, admired her for her life and her attitudes: they told him that you made medicines and that you had donated your beautiful hair. I urged her to tell him, listening to her was a lesson for him. Dr. Andrade is a good doctor, a good person, a husband and a father. With the knowledge of this episode, I hope he continues to be a humane and loving professional.

- He wasn't supposed to know. It was a joke! - exclaimed Noeli.

- Since Antero saw her, he thought her hair was beautiful.

He had in the past.

- Grandma, have Antero and I met before? - Noeli asked.

- As Noeli, you had many lovers. Antero, in his past life, was a romantic young man who loved to read, his dream was to study, but he couldn't because his family couldn't afford it. Everyone in the town knew the lady of the manor, and Antero, who had another name, fell in love with you and watched you from afar. Knowing that you went riding almost every morning, he followed you until one day you talked to him and...

Noeli remembered:

- I used to dress up for riding; sometimes my husband accompanied me, but most of the time I rode alone and met up with lovers. Antero knew about these meetings because he had been following me for some time. One morning, I talked to him, I found him interesting and, on our third date, we became lovers. It was fun for me, but Antero fell madly in love. We met for six months. Then I got pregnant, and I didn't know who the father was. I was very interested in João Luiz at the time. I decided to have an abortion and so I didn't ride for a while. Disgusted with my young lover, Antero, I broke up with him and he cried. I didn't care about his suffering. With both problems solved, I got rid of my lover and the child I was expecting, and dedicated myself to my husband's nephew. I heard that Antero fell ill and, months later, died.

- Antero - Maria continued - suffered a lot, he admired her hair too much; a romantic, he began to eat little and fell ill, didn't fight for his life and passed away. He was helped, studied on the spiritual plane and reincarnated with the aim of loving incarnate life, studying medicine and caring for the sick. He has succeeded, he is fulfilling what he planned. When Antero saw you in the square, he admired your hair, he thought it was beautiful and, over the years, whenever he remembered you, he remembered your hair. When he heard her in hospital talking about her love, he felt remorse for the joke; he had learned the lesson of not abusing feelings. He hadn't really thought that you would love him for one date.

- I hope I've also learned the lesson of not abusing other people's feelings! - exclaimed Noeli.

- I think, Maria concluded, that when we start to love each other, we no longer abuse feelings. You, like Noeli, didn't really love anyone, perhaps you liked João Luiz more. You wanted to enjoy yourself, you were reckless, many loved you; Thomas was passionate, and some lovers, like Antero, suffered for loving you and from your contempt.

- I had many loves before and, in this last incarnation, none! I rescued her, I suffered as I made her suffer! - exclaimed Noeli.

- That was an important lesson for you.

- Have I really learned?

- I'm sure you have, said Maria. - But if you doubt it, you'll have to pass a test.

- Grandma, maybe I'll have to be beautiful in my next incarnation. Beauty arouses interest, and I'll have to deal with it by being generous and not deceiving anyone. But I want so much, when I'm incarnate, to have love, get married and have children. How I'd love to be a mother!

- Noeli, you are here as a newly incarnate, you have a lot to learn on the spiritual plane. I can tell you one thing: you've redeemed your past mistakes through pain, you've learned your lesson and you've done good.

- Grandma, you were going to tell me about Nenvis, with whom you work. Tell me about your job, asked Noeli.

- Nenvis helped me, when I was incarnate, to make the medicines; at that time, with no doctors in the city, the poor had no one to consult, and there were few people who could afford to buy medicines, so our work was very important. When I disincarnated, I was helped, I learned many things and I continued with Nenvis helping incarnate people. That's how I was able to be with you and Violeta. This friend of mine loves medicines very much; he studied it when he was on the physical plane and perfected it when he was disincarnated. We are friends and kindred spirits. We love what we do.

- What is this work like? Do you help everyone? - Noeli wanted to know.

- The person who asks becomes receptive to receiving. We currently help those who are receptive. We have a lot of work to do.

- Grandma, I've been dreaming about flowers, sometimes I even feel them when I'm awake. I know that many plants are cultivated here in the colony, we even have our own little garden. This feeling is different, I don't understand it, it feels like the flowers are mine. And I've been feeling requests, like they're asking me for help. I don't understand and I'm afraid of upsetting myself.

- You don't run that risk, and won't get upset, said Maria. - I'll tell you what's going on. As I've already told you, when you said you'd like flowers at your wake, you received many, not only from Mariana's mother, but also from neighbors and customers. Your wake was full of flowers. Mariana got a lot better and became healthy, the illness disappeared: Mariana, her family and then everyone in town thought it was because of the wig, her hair, and started asking you for help. Nenvis, friends and I have been working to help those who ask.

- Grandma, do I understand you correctly? - Noeli asked. - People have been asking me for things, but it's you and Nenvis who have been helping them, and they think it's me? What help are you giving?

- We try to help with everything and we've been able to fulfill many requests. The important thing is to do it. Many teams from the spiritual plane work tirelessly, lovingly, in the name of God, Jesus, Mary and many saints. The work belongs to those who do it. We are the masters of our actions. It is a pleasure for Nenvis and me to serve people in your name. Many people have come to the cemetery to bring flowers to his tomb and ask for graces.

- These graces are all your work.

- Yes, agreed Maria.

- I think I have to go to the crust to see this, don't you?

- Dedicate yourself to studying for the moment; then I'll take you to see what we're doing: Nenvis, Carlos, Clara, Leocárcio and me. You will learn with us this way of operating, helping, which they have been asking you to do.

- Can't I go now? - Noeli asked.

- I want you to learn to fly safely, to feed yourself by nourishing yourself with the air, the sun and nature. Then we're waiting for Fr. Ambrózio to disincarnate: he's ill and will soon return to the spiritual plane.

- He can be helped, can't he? - Noeli wanted to know.

- Yes, Father Ambrózio deserves help. Many friends are waiting for him. He's a good person, he's practiced his priesthood trying to be fair and he's done charitable work.

- Grandma, what do I do when I feel the requests?

- Think of God, pray and do as João Luiz did: have a goal, study, learn so that, as soon as possible, you can be with us to help those who ask you, advised Maria.

- Grandma, Mariana had cancer; for the time being, on the physical plane, this disease cannot be cured. How did she heal?

- Firstly, she was very receptive; secondly, the medicine we have on the spiritual plane is much more evolved. Here we already know how to cure cancer. Disincarnates are studying, researching here, reincarnating, studying, researching and medicines are emerging: I think that soon many cancer patients will be cured, until everyone is cured.

- Then other illnesses appear, lamented Violeta's daughter.

- Diseases will exist until everyone understands that love is the most important thing. Because the spirit that loves no longer makes mistakes and becomes healthy, so a healthy spirit, a healthy body.

- This will surely happen in the future!

- We've made progress! - exclaimed Maria.

- I'm going to study a lot!

She began to accompany João Luiz on his courses. She studied a lot and, in the study where we learn to help incarnate people, they both understood that no one can interfere in another person's life, or babysit, or do the lesson that the incarnate person is supposed to do. Helping with wisdom requires great care.

Father Ambrózio disincarnated and, eight days later, Noeli and João Luiz went to visit him.

- My godson! What a pleasant surprise! - exclaimed Father Ambrózio. They talked for a few minutes.

- I was ill, said the priest, and I got worse. Doctor Daniel admitted me to hospital and I passed away with a lot of shortness of breath and chest pains. I'm fine here.

- Aren't you surprised you're not in heaven? - asked João Luiz.

- Isn't this heaven? Of course, it is. I always thought that heaven was the continuation of life, pleasant for people who have fulfilled their obligations.

- You're right, this is heaven, agreed João Luiz.

- I hope it's not eternal rest, said Father Ambrózio. - I don't like sitting around.

- Get ready then, there's a lot to do here - João Luiz laughed.

It was a pleasant visit.

Noeli continued to feel the flowers and the requests. When it was eight months since she had made her change of plan, Maria told her:

- Get ready, my granddaughter, you will go with me to the crust and help us fulfill the requests they make of you. You will work with us.

- I've thought about staying in the colony for several years, I love this place so much.

- You can come back as often as you like. You'll stay with us in an aid station that has been built over the hospital. You'll have your own corner there.

- João Luiz wants to work with incarnates and I'm the one who's going! - lamented Noeli.

- He'll soon be able to go too. Don't be afraid, you'll be with me and you'll learn a lot. Study becomes concrete when we put what we learn into practice.

Noeli said goodbye to the residents of the house, told them in her courses that she would be going away and hugged João Luiz, promising that they would see each other whenever possible. Her room would still be waiting for her when she came to the colony.

I'm going to miss all this, she thought. Seeing the sky in this shade of blue, the night, the stars, the plants and the people who live here...'

She left with her grandmother.

# Chapter 12

## *LEARNING TO HELP*

Noeli flew with Maria. It was a very pleasant feeling. Nearing the crust, they flew slowly. They approached the city where they had lived while incarnate and where they would be working.

- What a different feeling to see the city from up here! - exclaimed Noeli.

- I'm going to take you for a walk around the city. Look at the church, the square - showed Maria.

- Grandma, I'd like to see the manor house again, asked her granddaughter.

- There it is!

When she saw the manor house, Noeli was startled.

- The news of the expropriation has spread, explained Maria. - This is sure to happen and, knowing this, people have come here and taken away what could be useful to them. They took down the doors, the chicken coop screens, fences, tiles and bricks. Isn't it good that these things were useful?

- Yes, it is. What about the paintings and books? - Noeli wanted to know.

- The paintings have been taken down and stored because the town hall has plans to build a museum and, when that happens, they'll put them in it. Some of the books have been donated to the school and others have been kept.

Noeli looked at the old manor house. It was all ruins, broken down, walls in pieces, from above she could see the staircase and the floors.

Grandma's right, she thought, it's a good thing the materials in this house were reused. This manor house used to be a luxury, then a simple dwelling, and now it's a ruin.

We need to be careful not to let this happen to our lives.

- And now, Grandma, where are we going? - Noeli asked.

- To the aid station, where you'll be living for a while.

Maria, hand in hand with her granddaughter, headed for the hospital. The newcomer was amazed. The hospital known to the incarnate was being enlarged, and it was beautiful to see from above the construction of the building where the sick was housed.

- I see hospitals as places that relieve pain. - said Noeli.

- Look at the building above the one on the physical plane.

Noeli watched in amazement as she saw a building like the ones seen in the colonies. As if it were the upper floor, she saw a very beautiful building. It was at the entrance to this building that the two went downstairs.

- Let's go in, invited Maria. - Here's how I do it.

I put my hand through the peephole and the door opens.

- Why is that, Grandma?

- Unfortunately, replied Maria, there are more than just well-meaning people on planet Earth. By joining our team, you will see many differences between human beings. We have brothers and sisters who recklessly prefer another kind of life. The aid stations, the places that house the good and those who are being helped, still need to be protected because, for many reasons, disincarnates who don't know love try to invade.

- What are these reasons? - Noeli asked curiously.

- Many of them want to mess things up, others come here in search of disaffected people who are sheltered and receiving help, there are also those who come out of curiosity and others who are bothered by the tasks of the good ones. I don't want you to be alarmed: when we work helping incarnates, we come across heterogeneity, good people and others who are not so good. We see many disincarnate people and, among them, some who are disturbed, others who want revenge and some who are recklessly evil. Come and see this house of love.

Noeli went in and noticed the cleanliness and simplicity, a fact that caught her attention, as she had always loved cleanliness.

- This is the entrance hall, said Maria.

The newcomer looked around curiously. The space was small, there was only a desk with two armchairs. There was a painting on the right-hand wall and another on the left.

- On this board - Maria showed the one on the right - are the names of all the workers in the house; on this side, the names of the sheltered people. This is to make it easier to know who works and who is staying at this post.

- Grandma, is it easy to find someone on the spiritual plane? - Noeli asked.

- If the discarnate wants to be found, it's easy. The spiritual plane is immense and there are countless places where a survivor of the physical body can go or stay. Finding a disturbed discarnate is more difficult. These pictures make these encounters easier.

Maria opened a door and they were faced with a corridor:

- This is the cafeteria. Even if you don't eat, you might feel hungry after a lot of work. In this room, the workers can help themselves to the food that comes from the colony, and the people in the recovery phase take their meals.

Noeli observed everything: in the room, there were several tables and many chairs. They returned to the corridor.

- In this part - Maria opened another door - are our corners.

They came across a large room with several armchairs.

- This is where we rest - Maria told them - we listen to music; through this device, we hear news from the spiritual plane and some, the most important, from the physical plane. The group of helpers meets here to talk and exchange experiences. We have some rooms over there. I've reserved one for you. In our team, only Leocárcio still sleeps sometimes. I don't have a room: I keep some of my belongings in our house in the colony; others I leave here in a closet.

They passed a corridor and Maria opened a door.

- This is your room.

Noeli found a small room: it contained a bed, a closet, a desk and two chairs.

- How nice! I'm going to like it here.

- Let's go and visit the rest of the office, invited her grandmother.

They returned to the living room and there were two ladies, who were introduced to him.

- Lúcia and Mayara are house helpers, from this Raio do Sol Relief Post - explained Maria.

They hugged each other and both wished the newcomer a good stay.

Maria led her granddaughter back into the corridor.

- Following the corridor are the wards. On the left are the rooms for disincarnate women; those on the right house the men. Let's go into the first ward, where the better ones are: some of them will go to the colony, some will reincarnate, others will stay with us as helpers and, as soon as they learn to be useful, they will become workers.

Maria opened the door and they entered. A helper came to greet them.

- This is Marcília, a tireless worker at the house - said Maria.

Marcília hugged the newcomer and went back to her work. Noeli observed the place: the space was large, with several windows, many beds and, next to each bed, a bedside table and a chair; behind the headboard, there was a cupboard where the occupant of the bed could keep her belongings. On all the nightstands, there was a container of water, a glass, a lamp and then it varied: on some there were books; on others, photos, and on others still, fruit.

- Grandma, what belongings are in storage? I didn't bring anything. Do you keep anything?

- I have photos, books I've won, magazines and dried flowers. There are lots of things in these cupboards. Some sheltered women keep clothes, shoes, they like to change... There are also ornaments, books and lots of photographs.

- How is this possible? Pictures? - Noeli wanted to know.

- They were molded by the will of each one with the help of a worker who knows how to do this. They are replicas of what they had when they were on the physical plane. It usually softens the nostalgia to see portraits of family members.

Noeli thought she didn't change her clothes anymore because they didn't get dirty; as she never paid any attention to this detail, and because she felt comfortable in what she was wearing, she only put on one outfit when she left the hospital and kept it with her. She wasn't interested in having pictures or books, she would borrow them when she wanted to read. She had nothing and didn't feel like having anything.

Looking at everything, smiling and greeting everyone, Noeli saw a woman sitting with head down. She recognized her and exclaimed:

- Mrs. Pérola!

The woman raised her head and looked at her.

- Is that you, Stranger? I say: Moeni.

- Yes, it's me, Noeli. How are you?

- Better, replied Pérola. - Did you die? I mean: disincarnated? Has it been a while?

Noeli knew that the recently disincarnated and those being helped, when they feel better, ask a lot about it, they want to talk about disincarnating. Perhaps because they are worried about their own, they want to know how the other person has changed.

- I disincarnated, replied Violeta's daughter, a few months ago. I'm going to live here for a while, to learn how to be useful.

Noeli remembered that Pérola had disincarnated a few years ago, sat down on the bed next to her and held her hand.

- I suffered with my change of plane, said Pérola. I had hoped that my husband, who was older than me and ill, would die first. Unfortunately, I had made plans for my widowhood. But I was the one who passed away. I was very upset, I didn't understand, I didn't accept it and I stayed in my former home. I felt forgotten, the children had their own things to do, my husband had found a girlfriend and was feeling happy. How I suffered! One day, I remembered my house in this town; without understanding, I came to it. A former employee, also disincarnate, she is a worker at this post, came to visit me and asked if I didn't want to come to the hospital, I came with her and stayed in this part, I got better and understood that my physical body had died, that I needed to accept and learn to live with this body that survived. I'm being treated very well here, but I'm scared.

- Don't be afraid, Noeli asked. - Life really does go on. Please learn to live on the spiritual plane.

- Are you all, right? - asked Pérola.

- Yes, I'm fine. Disincarnation was a blessing for me.

- Not for me.

- Stranger, I'm sorry, I didn't mean to call you that.

- No need to apologize. My name is Noeli.

- I think, said Pérola, looking at her, that I need to apologize. I used to buy your things and I made a lot of money from them.

- I was grateful to you for buying them. The money from those objects was very useful to me.

- I could have paid you better - Pérola sighed.

- Mrs. Pérola, think of it as a business deal. Only you could buy them from me. I'm grateful for that. If it's good for you, I apologize and thank you.

- Thank you, Weir... I mean, Noeli.

Maria, while her granddaughter was talking, had gone to help Marcília and, when she saw the two of them hugging, she approached.

- Now we have to go.

The two smiled and said goodbye. Grandma and granddaughter returned to the corridor. Noeli stopped and asked:

- Grandma, was I wrong to sell the objects from the house?

- No, you didn't. First of all, you were the heiress; then Pietro gave them to you; he wanted you, disincarnate, to inherit everything, which at the time wasn't very much. He regretted his evil act and then for not having had the courage to take it over. And even if it hadn't been for this reason, that you were the owner's daughter, he wouldn't have done anything wrong either. The owner never heard from you again, he passed away, he no longer paid his employees, and the manor house no longer had an owner.

- I didn't expect to find Mrs. Pérola here, commented Noeli.

- Get ready, we're always seeing friends, family and acquaintances again, some in pleasant situations and others not so much.

- Mrs. Pérola apologize me.

- Here on the spiritual plane, Maria explained, we understand what happened more clearly. In fact, the only person in town who could afford to buy those objects was Pérola. For her, it was a business and she made a good profit, but it was also good for you. If you hadn't sold them, what would have become of them? You gave everything from the house to the neighbors across the street and, surely, because they didn't know the value of those pieces, they would have been discarded or used as mere utensils. I don't think there's anyone in town today who knows about rare and antique pieces. You were right to sell them.

- What will happen to Mrs. Pérola? If possible, I'd like to help her.

- She doesn't need any more help now, Maria replied. - She arrived here upset and feeling very ill. She'll soon be transferred to the colony to learn how to live disincarnated and I hope she'll be useful.

Maria took her to see the other wards; as Noeli had helped her mother in the infirmaries at the colony, she wasn't surprised to see people there and some of the workers she knew. The patients who were feeling very ill didn't recognize her. She chatted with some of them, giving them affectionate encouragement.

There, you've met the whole station! - exclaimed her grandmother.

- I remind you that you won't be working here, but you can go everywhere in this house of love. Let's go to the cemetery now. I've arranged with our team to take you there and see what's going on.

They drove off. They arrived at the cemetery and Noeli looked on in amazement.

- Grandma, how different this place is!

- You're seeing the same place on both planes! - Maria exclaimed. - As an incarnate, you used to see what was in dense matter. Now you're also seeing what's on the spiritual plane. There, in that small building, is a tiny aid station, where the disincarnated usually stay when they are disconnected from their dead bodies and receive first aid; some stay there for days, others for hours, some leave to wander and, unfortunately, there are those who return to their former homes, but the majority go to an aid station, as you saw in the hospital, or to the colonies.

- Does everyone who is buried here receive this aid? - Noeli asked.

- Unfortunately, no. Some are taken by those who hate them; others, by groups of troublemakers with whom they had an affinity when they were incarnate; a small percentage remain attached to the physical body for more hours or days. Those who deserve it are helped.

- Strange! Uhuu... Noeli turned to see who had called her. She saw three disincarnated people laughing.

They're disincarnating who usually wander around here, said Maria. - They usually come to the cemetery to have fun or enjoy the movement.

- How do they know me?

- You're known, you'll soon see why, and if you pay attention to the one who called you, you'll recognize him: he's Cida's son, the one who got drunk and was disincarnated when he fell off a bridge, he was drunk.

- Hi! Noeli greeted them, waving her hand. - How are you?

- What do I hear? Did the Stranger say hello? Hello!

We're fine, thank you.

- Let's go, my granddaughter, and see the shelter - Maria pulled her along.

The three disincarnated people watched the two and followed them, but a few meters away. Maria took her to see the aid station.

- Notice that around this building there is a soft bluish light, it's protection. The worker has already seen us and will turn it off so we can get inside. Let's get inside quickly because as soon as we pass, it will be switched on again.

- What happens if they don't turn it off? Would we get through? - Noeli wanted to know.

- We wouldn't. It's an insurmountable barrier.

- And the reason is the same as the aid station?

- Although, Maria replied, this place doesn't house any helpers for long, it has this protection so that it won't be attacked or invaded. This is where disincarnate people who like to riot usually hang out, and one way they amuse themselves is by disturbing the workers. Let's go in.

The two of them went in. The post was a hall, with no windows, only a door. There were six beds, eight chairs and a table.

- This is Sebastiana, she works as a first-aider here - Maria introduced herself.

After greeting her, Maria explained to her granddaughter:

- Darling, whenever you need to, you can come here, both to bring help and to take refuge or shelter if you feel threatened. Then I'll teach you how to turn off the device.

They said goodbye to Sebastiana, who turned off the protection and turned it back on as soon as they left.

- Usually, Maria explained, in almost every cemetery, there is a relief center and workers who help those in need. Depending on the size of the place on the physical plane, the spiritual shelter will be the same. Some are huge and there are many helpers working in them, others are medium-sized, and ours is small, like the one on the physical plane. However, all of them aim to give first aid to those being sheltered, but they don't stay for long.

- I didn't see any sheltered people, only one first-aider was there - commented Noeli.

- Sebastiana is always walking around the cemetery and the town; at the moment, she is waiting for her partner, who will bring two people in need.

- Even in a small place, there is a lot to do. There are many reckless people who disincarnate without preparation, without knowing anything about the change they will make. Let's go to the tomb where his remains are.

Noeli knew exactly where the tomb was and was amazed to see it.

- Grandma! How many flowers! Some dried, some withered, and these freshly picked. The whole tomb is covered in flowery bouquets!

- My granddaughter, our job these days is to fulfill the requests you make. And along with the requests, they offer flowers or bring them in gratitude, they pay promises.

- You and Mom didn't like promises, and I never made any.

- When you ask, you become receptive to receiving, said Maria. - The most important thing in this receptivity would be to try to change yourself for the better, to change vices for virtues. It didn't and won't make any difference to you to receive these bouquets. However, most people bring flowers with affection and gratitude. Nenvis is coming. I want you to meet him. He's our counselor.

A pleasant-looking man approached them both. Smiling, he hugged Maria's granddaughter.

- I wish you well with us, said Nenvis.

- I hope I'm not giving you any trouble, I'm an apprentice, said Noeli.

- We all are, he replied gently.

- My granddaughter, the people who have brought you flowers and some candles think you're a saint.

- Me? A saint?

- Yes, said Nenvis.

- But I'm not a saint! What does it mean to be a saint?

- I think, replied Nenvis, trying to clarify, that a saint is someone who is wise. If human beings had wisdom, they wouldn't make mistakes anymore. If they still make mistakes, it's because they lack understanding. I deduce that the one who makes mistakes is reckless and ignorant of universal, Divine truths, and the saint, the wise one, is the one who understands eternal truths, feels God in himself and sees the Creator in the other.

- So, ignorance usually leads to error, and wisdom to virtue? - Noeli asked.

- I think that's right, said the group's advisor. - A saint is one who has the knowledge of the Supreme Reality: of God. That's because those who truly feel God in themselves and in others start to live in the good and for the good and are no longer capable of making mistakes. Making mistakes leads to progress.

- I'm far from being a saint. They wrongly think I am one. Now what?

- We shouldn't care about the titles we're given, but what we can strive to be, replied Nenvis. - You'll be part of our team and, through our work, we've been striving to heal pain.

- I thank you for doing this work on my behalf. I don't even know how to help, but I'll learn. Do you know any saints?

- Don't be embarrassed to be called a "saint" or to think you're not. Yes, I know many wise spirits, some have been given this title, but most have not. I recently attended a lecture by a disincarnate who, in his last three incarnations, was given the title of "saint". He really is a wise spirit. I also know that, unfortunately, some who have received this title are not yet wise, and even others suffered when they made their moves to the afterlife.

- I didn't suffer! - exclaimed Noeli. - I'll try not to be embarrassed when I'm called this title that I'm far from worthy of. I feel that we have good energy here.

- All the incarnates who come here pray, clarified Nenvis. - Sincere prayers leave the place with benevolent and pleasant energies. Prayers with good feelings connect us to beneficial forces, to restorative energies. Although many come here to be served. Unfortunately, the proportion of those who want to be served is enormous. Those who serve are the minority.

- The world, said Maria, will only improve if we consciously stop being served and start serving.

- Does everyone who comes here receive these salutary energies? - asked Noeli.

- Unfortunately, no, replied Nenvis. - Those with bad thoughts don't receive good energies. When someone comes here with negative thoughts, the beneficial energies return to their source or remain here.

- The members of our team are arriving, said Maria, and they want to greet you. They've already met you in the flesh. I'll introduce them.

Noeli watched them, they came flying in. She felt she knew them; she was hugged and Maria introduced them:

- This is Clara, she disincarnated thirty years ago, she plans to reincarnate and become a doctor. She met Nenvis at a lecture and was invited to join our small team.

- Welcome, it's a pleasure to have you with us, said Clara, smiling.

- This is Leocárcio, Maria continued, he's only been disincarnated for a short time. You may remember him, he's Izildiña's husband, who used to go to get medicine, he lived on the other side of town.

Noeli didn't remember him, but Izildiña, and asked:

- How is Izildiña?

- It was to be close to her, replied Leocárcio, that I asked to work on the team. In my spare time, I visit her. She has a lot of problems, but with my help, care and encouragement, she faces them with courage. I'm glad you're with us. I'm also an apprentice.

- This is Carlos - Maria showed him.

Noeli looked at him, he was a handsome and friendly young man; he smiled and greeted her.

- I've been part of the team since Maria was making medicines. At the time, I was working with Nenvis in an aid station in a large hospital, he came to help Maria a few hours a week and I accompanied him. I really enjoyed working with herbs and took courses on the subject. Now I'm working here, continuing my studies at the colony and helping out at the city hospital. Welcome!

- Noeli, said Nenvis, you won't be alone at first. You'll always be with one of us, and you'll also rest for a few hours each day in your corner of the hospital's aid station. You'll see many good spirits working with us, and some not. You will also see those who suffer, although you have already seen them in the colony's hospitals. Unfortunately, you will encounter reckless and evil discarnate. You shouldn't be frightened or confront them; don't respond to their provocations.

- Do we get involved with them through our work? With these reckless ones? - Noeli wanted to know.

- The aim of our work at the moment is to help incarnates who ask for help and are therefore receptive to receiving it. You'll see that many of these assistances are laborious and, in some cases, we come up against obsessions, which can happen for many reasons. What gives us the most trouble is driving away vengeful spirits. Yes, in some of our tasks we come across discarnate spirits who call themselves "evil". In these cases, Carlos and I, because we have more experience, talk to them and try to help both the incarnated and the disincarnated.

- Of course, said Noeli, this task will be a great learning experience for me! I thank you and I hope I don't get in your way.

- Ask, my granddaughter, ask whenever you have any doubts, advised Maria.

Noeli looked at the discarnate people she had greeted, they were behind a tomb watching them and trying to listen.

- Don't you feel like helping everyone? Like those people over there? - Violeta's daughter wanted to know.

- Didn't you hear what we said? - said Nenvis. - We help those who are receptive, in other words, those who want to receive. Unfortunately, helping those who don't want to would be forcing them, and that doesn't usually work. We all have free will. Even when helping a receptive incarnate involving a discarnate, we only offer help to the latter; if they accept, the problem is solved; if not, we try to instruct the incarnate to get out of the reckless person's vibrational range so as not to receive their influence any more.

What a lot of work! Can I do it? - thought Noeli.

- Of course you can, my granddaughter, exclaimed Maria. - You're more capable than you think.

She understood that everyone there was listening to her thoughts.

Noeli had had lessons on the subject, but she still had a lot to learn; she smiled and determined:

- I'm going to pay more attention to what I think.

- We should always pay attention to our thoughts, recommended the team leader. - Whether we are incarnate or discarnate. We attract many things through our thoughts, whether bad or good. Optimistic thoughts bring us joy and give us good energy.

- Do we receive requests that don't go through? That is, that we can't interfere with? - Noeli asked.

- Many, replied Leocárcio. - Some want it to rain, others don't, some ask for their team to win and others pray for the other team to win.

- Unfortunately, explained Nenvis, we receive requests that we can't interfere with, but those who ask receive beneficial energies from us for praying and some we can help with what they really need. There are many interesting cases.

- Are you ready to start working, Noeli? - Clara asked. - I see incarnates approaching with flowers.

Noeli smiled and looked towards the entrance to the cemetery.

# Chapter 13

# *AN INTERESTING CASE*

Two ladies approached the tomb, decorated with flowers. They were talking:

- Thank you for coming with me, Clotilde. I'm afraid to come to the cemetery alone. I came to pay my promise. Little Saint did what I asked.

- Is it right, Maria Luiza, to call her Little Saint?

- Oh, Clotilde, what should I call her? Strange Saint? It's certainly disrespectful. Saint Sophia? Sofia wasn't her name. By her real name, which is so different and few people pronounce correctly? Little Saint is affectionate. Let's put the flowers in. Little Saint, I've come to pay my promise. My husband has improved a lot.

- What if it's temporary, if your husband becomes aggressive again?

- Then I'll ask Little Saint again. - Let's pray. The two placed the flowers on the grave and prayed.

Noeli was curious, and Maria enlightened her.

- Maria Luiza's husband was very nervous and aggressive, and she asked us for help. We went to his home and saw that the cause of the quarrel was his disincarnate brother. This spirit had been on the spiritual plane for eight years and had even been helped, but he didn't want to be sheltered, so he left and wandered around. He liked staying with his brother. This spirit, when incarnate, was authoritarian and began to give his opinion on Maria Luiza's husband's life. The disincarnate wanted his brother to be authoritarian too and treat his wife unkindly. We talked to this spirit, trying to convince him that he was doing the wrong thing. We took him to a help center far from here and put him to do a task that he liked, so we took him away from this home. We talked to the couple while their physical bodies slept, asking them to be patient with each other and we told the husband that he should no longer call out for his brother or accept him around. Peace returned to the home.

The two ladies left.

- Does everyone pay their promises? - Noeli wanted to know.

- We don't pay attention to that, Nenvis replied. - I think most of them do. I see this as an act of gratitude. Those who are grateful are learning to love, and those who are grateful are open to always receiving. It makes no difference to us whether they pay or not. However, for some people who haven't kept their promises, this attitude can upset them, because they haven't done something they set out to do. They could just as well ask, become receptive, without promising anything in return.

A little girl approached the grave. Noeli watched her; the girl was carrying a tiny flower. Her clothes were torn, in some places mended, and she wasn't clean, her hair was matted. The girl timidly placed the little flower in the right-hand corner of the slab.

Hail Mary, she thought, and everyone on the team listened, help us. I know you're close to God and can solve our problems. Hail Mary...

- This little girl is twelve years old, said Carlos, because she's anemic and going through a lot of deprivation.

- What is she really asking for? - asked Noeli.

- I'm sure she's asking for help for her troubled family, said Nenvis, and ordered: Noeli and Carlos, accompany her and try to help her in any way you can.

- She brought me a small flower. - Noeli was moved, and tears streamed down her face when she saw the girl crying.

- My granddaughter, Maria advised, most requests cause us to be moved. Feeling pity without doing anything is useless.

- But I want to help her!

- Then make an effort, Maria advised. - I'm sure you and Carlos will help this girl.

The girl hurried off, Carlos and Noeli followed her and heard the girl thinking:

- I have to get back quickly; otherwise, Grandma will be angry. And when she finds out that I took the flower from her plant, I might get slapped. I hope she hasn't been drinking. I still have a lot to do. I'm tired. The slaps Grandma gave me last night still hurt.

The girl walked quickly; after about twenty minutes, she came to a simple little house.

A lady was sitting on a chair and, when she saw the girl, asked:

- Where did you go, Gloriña? Have you done your laundry?

Carlos and Noeli learned that the girl was called Gloriña.

- I soaked it, I'm going to wash it, replied the girl.

- Where did you go?

- To the cemetery, to ask Little Saint for help.

- Useless girl! - exclaimed the lady. - Do you believe that an ugly woman like the Stranger can work miracles? What can she do for us? Give your mother some sense? Rich food for us? You're an insufferable girl! Everyone who orders brings flowers, and what did you bring?

The lady looked at the vase where the little flower used to be and shouted:

- Did you take the flower from the vase? You thief! I'll hit you!

She raised her arm to strike Gloriña. Carlos held her arm and stared at her. He said:

- Don't hit her!

The lady lowered her arm and sat down again. Gloriña ran to the sink and started washing.

- You managed to interfere. You stopped the lady from hitting the girl. How did you do that? - Noeli was curious.

- It's very difficult for a disincarnated person to interfere in cases like this. This woman didn't feel that I was holding her arm. It was an instinctive act I did, perhaps that's why I concentrated all my energy, and this lady felt something different.

- I'm glad you made it. Gloriña was going to be beaten for taking the flower to my grave.

They entered the house and approached the lady, two reckless discarnate, they were laughing, they didn't see the two rescuers because they were in different vibrations.

Reckless discarnate see others like themselves and the incarnate.

- So, Geralda, shall we take our first doses? - asked one of them.

- Your name is Geralda, said Noeli.

- Take the brandy and put it in the mug! - ordered the other disincarnate.

- There's a bad vibe in here, observed the first one who spoke. - I don't like it. What could it be?

- Has the girl gone to ask the Stranger for help?

- She said she was going yesterday. We'd better get going.

Shall we go to the bar?

They left. Geralda didn't drink, she picked up the broom and started sweeping the house.

- What a thing! Can't you sleep in this house anymore?

A woman opened the bedroom door, she was only in her underwear. Noeli looked at her, she must not have been thirty, she was beautiful.

The two women started arguing.

They were mother and daughter. The language was rude. The two rescuers learned that the woman's name was Doralice and that she was the mother of Goriña and two boys who were at nursery school.

- Geralda is an alcoholic, said Carlos. - Doralice, as well as drinking, has been using drugs, is a prostitute and doesn't pay any attention to her children. Watching them, I can see their physical bodies being bombarded by the toxins of alcohol and drugs. Let's get closer to Goriña.

The girl washed the clothes, then put them on the clothesline and went to help her grandmother make lunch. She ate very little.

- Let's go, decided Carlos, I'll tell Nenvis what we've seen here and plan the best way to help Gloriña.[10]

- We followed the girl, whose name is Maria da Glória. Her home is unstructured, her maternal grandmother is drunk and violent, and her mother is an alcoholic who is also using drugs at the moment. Doralice, the mother, has two small children aged five and two.

- Carlos, try to help these children, and Noeli will be your helper, asked the group's advisor.

In the afternoon, the two rescuers returned to the house. Gloriña was getting ready to pick up her siblings from nursery school. The girl walked quickly, not even looking around. She was tired. She had worked hard. But she smiled when she saw her brothers. The two boys were dressed simply and smiled back. Hand in hand, they returned home, now walking slowly. The nursery school was close to the house. Grandma and mom weren't there, and the boys had already showered. They sat on the floor and played with the baby carriage. There was very little food for dinner, so Gloriña gave it to her siblings and ate only the leftovers. She preferred to stay hungry. At twenty o'clock, she put her brothers to bed, the three of them sleeping in one bed. The house had one room and three beds: one belonged to her grandmother and

---

[10] N.A.E.: There were several jobs they were doing at the same time. Carlos and Noeli left Gloriña's home to come back later and, in the meantime, they went to do another task, to fulfill another request. I'm going to describe the help with a beginning, middle and end to make it easier to understand. When the group gathered at the aid station, Carlos told Nenvis what they had seen at the girl's home.

the other to her mother. Gloriña prayed and went to sleep too, and the three of them soon fell asleep.

Carlos took his companion to a bar not far from the house. They saw Geralda with a group of incarnate people, all drinking and laughing, and many disincarnate people beside her; they saw the two who had gone to her house in the morning. Doralice was talking to a man, they approached and listened:

- I told you, I'm going to pay you. On Saturday, I'll be seeing my clients from the farm. I'll pay you!

- I'm getting tired of you. Your debt is mounting. Why don't you sell your children? If your daughter wasn't so weak and skinny, I'd like her. I like girls!

Doralice didn't get upset. They argued for a few more minutes, then she went to do a show.

- I'm shocked! Oh my God! - exclaimed Noeli.

- They're reckless reincarnates, said Carlos. - From what I understand, Doralice has a big debt, it must be for the drugs. Let's get out of here.

They went to the aid station and planned what they would do.

- I'm remembering Mrs. Esmeralda, said Carlos, she's a seamstress and welcomes many women into her home. She's already helped us on other occasions. This lady is charitable and very religious, she receives our intuition easily.

Let's go to her house and ask her to help us.

They went to her house and Noeli liked Esmeralda. Her house was simple and welcoming. The two rescuers were about to leave when Doralice arrived, bringing some fabric to make a dress. She paid for the work in advance because if she didn't, Esmeralda wouldn't get paid. The children's mother complained to the seamstress that life was difficult with her children, and Esmeralda told the customer what Carlos wanted.

- Why don't you give your children away? There are people who want to adopt.

- Yes, that's fine, replied Doralice.

And it was Esmeralda too who remembered Doralice when she saw a customer and heard that her daughter-in-law couldn't have children and wanted to adopt.

- The children, two boys, aged five and two, are beautiful! I think she'll give them away, especially if she offers some money. She's in debt, said the seamstress.

When the woman arrived home, she informed her son.

Carlos and Noeli went to visit the couple and realized that they were good people who would love and care for the children.

The two rescuers worked hard to fulfill Gloriña's request. They had many conversations with the incarnate people involved. And something happened that helped the two workers. One of Doralice's bar companions disincarnated.

- She died - another bar-goer told Doralice - she was sick, she fainted and they took her to hospital. She was complaining of abdominal pains, and they said she had died of a liver disease, from getting too drunk.

Doralice thought she was in pain too, and it was a disincarnated companion of hers, with whom she used to do drugs, who helped them.

- Dora, my dear, I think you're going to die soon. It's better to sell your children. With the money, you can pay off your debts and enjoy the rest of your days!

Doralice, used to receiving intuition from this disincarnate, thought about it a lot.

The couple had come to town to try to adopt the children.

- Maybe she won't give them up, said the woman who wanted to be a mother.

- But she certainly will if we offer her money, said the husband. - But the boys are already grown up, five and two years old. Will it work?

- I've been thinking, said the wife, it's even better, newborns are a lot of work. Let's go and see them; if we like them, we'll ask their mother to talk to Doralice.

The couple went to the nursery, met the children and found them beautiful.

- With good treatment, these spots on their faces will disappear. They'll be healthy with a good diet. I want them both for my children, said the woman.

His mother, the boy who wanted to be a father, went to Doralice's house in the afternoon. Geralda wasn't there. The children's mother opened the door.

- Doralice, I want to talk to you, she said. - I'll get straight to the point. I have acquaintances, rich people, a couple who live far from here, who want to adopt their two children. They pay for them... - said the amount.

Doralice got excited and thought:

- As well as cutting down on household expenses, with what I get, I'll pay off my debts and I'll still have money for a long time. None of the three children has a father, I don't know who they are. They're mine alone and I do what I want.

He asked for a bit more, they negotiated. The woman paid.

- I'm going to pick them up from nursery, I don't want to take anything from them, the kids will have everything new, good things. They'll be well looked after.

The woman left. Gloriña was in the bedroom and heard everything.

When I can, she thought, I'll take flowers to Little Saint. She's the one who must be helping. What I wanted most was for my little brothers to have a home, a father and mother to look after them and for them not to go hungry any more. Will they really be all right? Little Saint, look after my brothers for me. Please!

Noeli approached Gloriña, hugged her affectionately and tried to calm her down.

- Gloriña, calm down! - Noeli asked. - Your siblings will be fine; they'll have a home. Their adoptive parents are good people, they will be loved, brought up well and will study.

The girl cried, and the first-aider struggled not to cry. Doralice shouted for her daughter.

- Maria da Glória! Gloriña!

The girl wiped her face and went into the living room.

- As you may have heard, I've given you your brothers. Good for you! You won't have to pick them up from nursery or look after them and you'll have a bed to yourself.

- I won't see them anymore? - Gloriña asked.

- No, we won't see them anymore, replied Doralice.

- I'm going to the nursery to make sure they really aren't there.

I wonder if the lady won't pick them up, thought Doralice. If she doesn't, I won't give the money back. I really won't. She must have gone to get them.

- Fine, go at the usual time, agreed Doralice.

- I'm going to iron clothes, said the girl.

- Don't iron your brothers' clothes. If you go to pick them up and they're not there, give them all their clothes, toys, everything.

Carlos and Noeli went to the nursery, and the lady who had spoken to Doralice went to pick up the boys. Their mother wrote a note giving her permission to take them. The children looked frightened at the woman, and she spoke affectionately:

- Children, I've brought you some lollipops. I'm taking them for ice cream. Your mother let me.

- Gloriña did? - asked the older boy.

- Yes, she did.

The woman, seeing how excited the boys were about the lollipops, spoke quietly to the principal.

- Doralice, their mother, gave them to me. Please get their birth certificates, she told me they're here. The two of them won't be returning to the nursery. A couple from a city far away will adopt them.

With the boys' documents, the lady left.

The two rescuers accompanied them. At the house, the couple were overjoyed to see them.

- We're leaving early tomorrow, decided the adoptive mother

- I'm going to buy them lots of clothes and toys; I'm going to do everything I can to please them at first, so that they don't feel strange, I'm going to take them to the doctor and the dentist. I already love them both!

The father agreed and was amazed to see them eating, they ate a lot.

- What about Gloriña? - the older boy wanted to know.

- She's very happy that you're going to live in a big house with lots of toys, said the lady.

The maid arrived with lots of packages. She had gone to buy clothes and toys. The little boys were thrilled with the presents.

- They'll be fine, said Carlos. - The couple already love them.

They returned to Gloriña's home. At the usual time, the girl went to the nursery and was told that her brothers had left. She returned home and her mother was waiting for her.

- So? They've gone?

- Yes, they did.

Then Geralda arrived.

- Where are the children? Lazy girl, didn't you go and get them? Go now!

- Grandma, I went, they weren't there. Mom traded them with a lady.

- I gave them to her, said Doralice. - A woman is going to take them to a big city. A couple will adopt them. They've even said they'll change their names. My children will be fine.[11]

---

[11] N.A.E.: In the time and place where this happened, adoption was easier.

- You really suck. No matter how hard I had to work, I didn't give you away. How much did you get? Half is mine!

The two women started arguing, Gloriña ran into the bedroom and cowered in the corner of the bed. The two women even slapped each other, shouted and cursed. Doralice gave money to her mother, who left again, surely going to pay off some debts and get drunk. Gloriña's mother counted the money.

With this, I'll pay off my debts; with this, I'll have a party tonight; and I'll keep this package. I'll have money for a few months.

- Gloriña, Doralice called, eat all the food, your grandmother has left and I'll be leaving soon. Would you like a drink? I'll make it for you with lemon and sugar.

- No, I don't want to, replied the girl.

- All right, but don't be sad. Your brothers will be fine. I'll get ready.

This girl, thought Doralice, is very skinny and ugly. She could give me some money in a pinch. I could sell her to a drug dealer who likes girls.

She went to get ready. Noeli couldn't hold back her tears.

Carlos was calm.

- I'm going to give the girl some energy. Then we'll see if we can get her into another home.

The two rescuers continued to help.

Again, they went to the seamstress and insisted.

- Don't you know who could take Doralice's girl?

At night, when the seamstress slept, the two talked to her, her perispirit moving away from her sleeping body.

- Couldn't you help us? We want to find a home for Gloriña, Doralice's daughter, asked Noeli.

- I've been thinking a lot about this little girl. I'm distracted by sewing and suddenly I think of her. What can I do?

- Ask around. You know lots of people. Maybe someone would like to keep her.

The other day, the seamstress asked her customers, acquaintances and neighbors. One lady was interested, but Carlos and Noeli didn't like it, because this lady thought:

- That girl is a hard worker, she looks after her brothers, she does all the housework. Gloriña can come to my house as a maid. Of course, she'll be better off, she'll eat and she'll have clothes.

Instructed, the seamstress asked why she was interested and didn't like the answer.

It's not fair for the girl to go from bad to worse. I'll keep looking.

And she did: she was a well-known woman, a retired teacher, who was going to live alone because her only daughter was getting married. Esmeralda went to talk to her.

- Of course - said the seamstress to the retired teacher - the girl must be anemic, she's skinny, she needs a home, her grandmother and mother get drunk and mistreat her. If you want to keep her, my son, who is a police sergeant, will take her out of the house and bring her here.

- I was afraid of being alone. I think God is helping me. I'll help the girl and she'll keep me company. I'm going to talk to my daughter.

Once again, Carlos and Noeli talked to mother and daughter while their physical bodies were asleep. The daughter liked the idea; with her mother not being alone, she would be more at ease. The lady liked the company and took pity on the girl.

With everything settled, the seamstress's son went to Doralice's house when the three of them were home.

- This girl can't live here anymore, said the policeman. - She's mistreated; everyone knows that you two beat her. For this mistreatment, I can arrest you. As I'm a good person, I won't arrest you, but I will take the girl. And I warn you not to go after her. The law protects the girl. If you harass her, I'll arrest both of you.

Geralda and Doralice, having committed many reckless acts, feared the police. Out of fear, they didn't say anything. They knew they weren't doing the right thing by the girl. They didn't even try to find out if the policeman was doing the right thing.

Esmeralda's son did this only with the intention of helping. He certainly wouldn't be able to do that nowadays. The procedure would certainly be different.

Gloriña was frightened, the policeman smiled at her and Noeli tried to calm her down.

- Girl, pack your clothes and come with me! - ordered the sergeant.

Gloriña did so quickly, saying goodbye to her grandmother and mother. The policeman took her to the retired teacher's house. Mother and daughter took pity when they saw her. They lovingly cared for her wounds and her hair and, a week later, she looked better. The doctor prescribed vitamins, the dentist started treating her teeth, she got new clothes. She was very happy, but she was afraid that her mother would come for her.

Geralda and Doralice were really afraid of being arrested and decided not to go after Gloriña. Carlos and Noeli didn't visit them anymore, and the two continued to get drunk.

Seeing that the seamstress had muscle pain from the repetitive gestures of her work, Carlos helped her.

- It's a pleasure to help those who help us! - exclaimed Carlos.

Her pain improved.

Doralice died five years later, murdered in a fight, and Geralda went to a nursing home.

The two children really got on well, grew up healthy and were loved by their adoptive parents.

The lady gave Gloriña lessons and enrolled her in school. She became healthy, polite, attentive to her guardian, and the two liked each other very much, becoming great friends. Gloriña trained as a teacher and became a schoolmaster. With her first paycheck, she bought flowers, took them to Noeli's grave and thanked her for the help she had received. She also bought clothes and food and took them to her grandmother in the nursing home.

- Did you bring any alcohol? - asked Geralda. - No? Ungrateful granddaughter! Take it all back.

But you took it all. Geralda didn't say thank you. Gloriña felt sorry for her grandmother and started taking things back to her every month. This was the task that Noeli was most moved by, perhaps because it was her first job, and she always remembered it in detail.

# Chapter 14
## *OTHER TASKS*

Noeli was learning a lot as part of the team. The group helped by healing pain, counseling and guiding those who asked them for grace. They were also always at the hospital, intuiting doctors Daniel and Antero, who usually received the intuitions when diagnosing the illnesses of the beggars. Many of the requests involved residents of the spiritual plane. They were disincarnated people returning to their former homes, upsetting themselves and, consequently, disharmonizing their families. When this happened, they talked to the spirits, showing them the disadvantages of wandering aimlessly, that they were harming themselves and those they loved. Some of the cases were easier, the survivors on the physical plane understood and accepted the help offered, and went to the aid station. Others were more difficult: they didn't want to leave their family, their home and, sometimes, the material possessions they mistakenly thought were theirs. And many of these people only stayed for a short time; feeling better, they left without permission. It was also necessary to insist that the incarnate not call their discarnate loved ones, not to ask them for anything, because when they did this, the newly-arrived person, feeling called, asked, would end up answering them and, without permission, not knowing how to help, would get upset again, and the disharmony would continue in the home.

- How different it is when the family doesn't despair at their loved one's move and, through prayers and good thoughts, helps them adapt to the new way of life! - exclaimed Noeli.

A mother, accompanied by her seventeen-year-old son, visited the cemetery with flowers to ask for help. The boy, Frederico, was thin and haggard and was undergoing medical treatment. Listening to the mother, the team learned that the young man had been fainting for eight months, becoming ill, sometimes vomiting and, on these occasions, talking and no one understanding what he was saying. After the crisis, Frederico remembered nothing. He was eating very little, had lost a lot of weight and was afraid to sleep. The doctor had prescribed a lot of medication.

- He's being obsessed, Nenvis diagnosed. - The discarnate who is making him ill is just over there, at the entrance to the cemetery. Maria, Carlos, give him and his mother passes, encourage them to pray. Come with me, Noeli, I'm going to talk to this discarnate who is currently an obsessor. I'm sure you'll learn a lot from listening to us. If we don't lower our vibration, this spirit won't see or hear us. I will change my vibration; I will look coarser. Not you, you will only listen in order to learn.

Noeli followed the team leader. She marveled at her transformation: her perispirit took the form of a tall, thin man with a beard down to his chest, red hair, and coarse clothes.

- I looked like that in one of my incarnations. You only have to remember it and want to change yourself to make this transformation. This is because I have learned.

They approached the disincarnate, who was attentive, looking at mother and son.

- Good afternoon. How are you? - Nenvis greeted the disincarnate, who was startled.

Noeli observed him: he appeared to have disincarnated at the age of forty. He must have been handsome, but the expression of hatred and resentment had changed his per spiritual appearance: his eyes were red, his lips were clenched, his hair was dirty and tangled, and he wore dirty black clothes. He didn't see Noeli; he looked at Nenvis and asked:

- Who are you? I don't know you and I don't talk to people I don't know.

- I'm Nenvis. That's it! Now we know each other. What's your name?

- Nenvis? Strange name.

- It's a surname. Everyone knows me like that.

- My name is Charles. I used to be important.

- What are you looking at? The little saint's tomb? Are you going to pray to her? - asked the team leader.

- Can discarnate people also ask?

- Of course! We're all alive, replied Nenvis.

- I'm going to ask Little Saint not to listen to that mother and her son.

- Don't you like them?

- I don't like her because she's, his mother. I hate Marguerite! - replied Charles.

- Marguerite? The boy's name is Frederico.

- You know things. Why is that? Is he an intruder? Do you want to be imprisoned on the threshold? I'll tie you up and take you there.

- I'm not an intruder, I'm curious.

- Of course, I know that her name is Frederico now. Margarida was the name she used in her other existence. She did me a lot of harm and hid in a male body, said Charles.

The conversation was long. In front of the tomb, mother and son prayed a rosary. By praying, Charles and Maria were able to remove the negative energy surrounding them and give them the beneficial one, so they both felt better. Nenvis told Charles that he wandered around and liked to talk. Charles told him that, in Frederico's previous incarnation, he had been a woman and had done him a lot of harm. She seduced him, made him murder his wife to keep her and, soon after they married, betrayed him. He angrily murdered Margarida when he found out she was running off with someone else. He said he suffered a lot for being despised and betrayed and blamed her for making him a murderer. He disincarnated due to illness, suffered in the umbral zone, and this only increased his hatred for her. When his disturbance improved, he went looking for her, took a long time to find her and was surprised: Margarida had reincarnated as a man. He thought that his wife from the past had been hiding from him.

- Now that I've found her, Charles said, I'm going to punish her!

Nenvis remained calm, looking at him. The obsessor grew drowsy and fell asleep. The group leader picked him up.

- I'm going to take you to a place, a spiritualist center, and you'll be guided in a meeting. Come with me!

Noeli was excited; she wanted to see a place where Allan Kardec's guidelines were followed. The place on the physical plane was simple: chairs, a table and a bookcase. Above, there was a building on the spiritual plane, a help center. A disincarnated worker from the place welcomed them and greeted them happily. Nenvis explained the reason for his visit.

- I've come to bring a disincarnate who only thinks about revenge. Charles needs help and clarification.

- Charles, said the aid worker, will stay with us asleep in one of our beds until tomorrow night, when we have the orientation meeting. Let's talk to him.

Nenvis told the worker what was happening and added.

- In his past incarnation, Frederico's mother was Charles' first wife, who was murdered by him. In this incarnation, she has taken her husband's former lover as her son and loves him very much. One of Frederico's brothers was his son.

Leaving him asleep, they said goodbye. Noeli, curious, asked:

- How do you know this?

- After many years of helping people, I've learned a lot. Sometimes you just have to observe carefully to know a lot about a spirit. I saw Frederico and his mother praying, I observed them and also Charles. I didn't do this out of curiosity, but to help everyone involved in this help we intend to do.

For other reasons, Nenvis and Noeli didn't go to the meeting. The next day, they went to the spiritualist center to talk to Charles. They found him very sad.

- Charles, do you remember me? I'm Nenvis, a disincarnate who works trying to help people who go to ask for graces for Little Saint. Frederico and his mother asked.

When I saw you accompanying them, and talked to you, I wanted to help you and brought you here.

- I was so focused on getting revenge that I didn't think about anything else, said Charles. - I forgot that I murdered my first wife, that I separated her from our three children. I only looked for Marguerite, the woman I loved and who despised me, my enemy, and I didn't care about those I loved and who loved me. It was a great surprise when, helped by the kind workers in this house, I came to know who the people are who are by her side. Frederico's mother was my wife in the past; she was honest and good and, in this incarnation, she accepted my lover as her son. By harming him, she was mistreating the whole family. His mother is again very dedicated, she is worried and suffers when she sees her son ill. My son, whom she loved very much, is now her son again and another man, a good father and excellent husband, the partner she deserves. The whole family, especially the parents, are worried to see Frederico ill.

- The worst thing, Charles, is what I was doing to you, said Nenvis.

- What do you mean "with me"? - Charles asked.

- I remember, when I was incarnate, two neighbors. They were both seamstresses. One was dedicated to her work and to learning more and more about her craft. The other, curious, loved to know what was happening to people, kept an eye on her neighbors and gossiped. The first was successful and the other was not. The second eventually realized that she was taking more care of other people's lives than her own, that she had wasted time, and that time is precious. You, Charles, have studied on the spiritual plane, you know many colonies, aid stations, you've made many friends, you play the piano perfectly and...

- Not at all. You're wrong, Charles interrupted.

- Oh, yes! You took care of someone else's life and forgot yours! When, Charles, we look after our own lives, then good things happen to us. You made a mistake and chose to blame your mistakes on your neighbor. We should all take responsibility for the wrongs we've done. You should have asked for forgiveness and taken care of your life.

- I understood. I didn't have to kill my first wife or my second. I'm a murderer! I understand that now. I focused on what I received and not on what I did. I wasted time. Instead of taking care of my life, I wanted to control her life, which I still love, and maybe that's why I felt so much resentment.

- You still have time. Charles, seize the opportunity, go learn to be useful, do-good things and get ready to be reincarnated. Take care of yourself without forgetting to do good to others. Because all our actions belong to us.

Charles thanked her and was determined to make the most of the opportunity. Nenvis and Noeli said goodbye and went back to their work.

- Won't Charles go back to Frederico? - she asked.

- I don't think so. That's because he was moved to learn that Frederico's mother was his first wife. This was a great example to him and to us. This woman is certainly a progressing spirit. Frederico will improve, let's encourage him to pray. Because even without Charles' presence, this young man has a lot to learn and redeem. He was very frivolous in his previous incarnation and committed many evil deeds.

Frederico and his mother returned to the cemetery to say thank you. He had improved, he was feeling better again.

Charles really understood, went about his life and never came near him again.

Every time they completed a task, succeeded in fulfilling their prayers, Noeli felt happy. They were working all the time. There were many people in need.

One fine Sunday morning, a girl praying in front of the tomb caught Noeli's eye. Nenvis was with her, the others were trying to solve another problem.

- What a coincidence! - exclaimed Mary's granddaughter.

- Yesterday a man, a widower with two small children, came here to ask me to help him find a good girl to marry and help him with his children. And today Maria Isabel is here asking for a husband! I wanted to help her!

- Perhaps we can unite, said Nenvis, the widower and this girl. First, let's see if she's a good person and if she could be a dedicated stepmother. I would like, as we always do, to help with the well-being of everyone involved, especially the children.

Noeli wanted to help Maria Isabel find a home. She lived with her brother and sister-in-law. She dreamed of having her own home, husband and children. Clara checked to see if she would be good for the orphans. She was pleased to see that Maria Isabel was a good person and incapable of evil. They went to visit the widower's family. His wife, who had died, had been helped and was recovering, but she was worried about her children. She wanted them to be well. The children's father was also a good person and it was difficult for him to work and look after the children. They had arranged to go to the cemetery on Sunday morning to bring flowers to the grave of their wife and mother. Clara did everything she could to get Maria Isabel to go to the cemetery at the same time, and she did. They met. The little girl, the widower's daughter, fell and Maria Isabel went to help her. The two adults introduced themselves and talked about the children. The four of them left the cemetery and went for ice cream. They exchanged information about each other while the children played in the playground.

The widower asked Maria Isabel out for the evening and she accepted. After this encounter, they started dating and, eight months later, they got married. They both paid their dues. Despite the usual problems that incarnate people face, the couple and their children lived better and had many moments of joy.

Another case that also struck Noeli was that of another mother who had come to pray for her son. Her plea was:

- Little Saint, help us! I have eight children and one of them was born handicapped. His birth was difficult and the boy had cerebral palsy. We look after him with love, I love him a lot, perhaps more than the others, because he's sick. I know he won't heal, that's not what I'm asking. My Nene, that's what we call him, seems to be upset lately. I think the Devil is messing with him, making him restless. Please help us!

- Let's go to this lady's house and see what's going on, said Nenvis. - She lives in another city; she came here just to ask for your help.

Nenvis, Carlos, Maria and Noeli went. The house was simple and, as Violeta's daughter noticed, clean. A child was lying on the sofa in the living room. He was small, thin, moved only his head and eyes, didn't speak, but listened. One of his sisters was feeding him, pouring broth into his mouth, and he was drooling.

- Nenê - commented Nenvis - is certainly recovering, through pain, the imprudence committed in the past. Let's give him a pass. Reckless discarnate must be surrounding him with negative energies.

The four rescuers concentrated and annulled the malevolent energies of the boy and the house, enveloping them with beneficial energy. Nenê stopped drooling and ate better.

Three disincarnate people, disharmonized by bad feelings, soon entered the house. Two men and a woman, who was very upset.

Talking to the disincarnates' involved in this obsession, they learned that, in Nene's past incarnation, he had been a wealthy landowner. Addicted to gambling, he lost a lot of money and ended up bankrupt. He lived in a huge house on a farm with his parents and a brother. Fearing bankruptcy, he planned to kill his mother, father and brother and then commit suicide. He murdered his parents in their sleep. His brother woke up and fought him, but was killed. With the noise of the fight, an employee, who was the property's watchman, saw what was happening and was also killed. A maid was also killed trying to help the watchman. And, as planned, she killed herself. Everyone involved was upset by the disincarnation and suffered. For the parents, it was a very painful change of plan, and they were very disappointed to learn that their son had murdered them. However, they eventually understood, they forgave and were helped. The brother and the employee didn't forgive and kept the ex-employee, who was very upset, with them.

The first to receive help was the woman, who accepted help. The most difficult was the ex-employee. When he was incarnate, he had committed many wrongful acts, killed two people and felt a lot of hatred. The disincarnate who had been Nenê's brother, after many conversations with the group and having been to the Spiritism center three times and received guidance, decided to forgive. He found the Gospel passage in which Jesus forgives his tormentors very beautiful. He also remembered his other incarnations and learned that he had been a murderer. He was taken to an aid station far away and planned to learn how to live on the spiritual plane and be useful.

The ex-employee gave the team more work, and for eight months they visited Nenê's home every day. The boy improved, was more relaxed and fed better.

- You, said Nenvis to the obsessor, you know well what disincarnating and reincarnation are. We all go through these processes. You suffered when you disincarnated. Have you ever thought that you will have to return to the physical plane? You've been following what happened to Nenê. He put on a body of flesh again. You also know that he suffered a lot when he came to the spiritual plane as a murderer and suicide bomber. He is now reincarnated and, as planned, he will only be in this sick body for a few more years and, when he disincarnates again, he will be helped this time. Because of the suffering he is going through, he will balance out and become healthy again. What will you do next? You're only focused on taking revenge. You have no goal. Will you be reincarnated? What will your return to dense matter be like?

- I don't want to be reincarnated! - exclaimed the obsessor loudly.

- Do you have power over this? Reincarnation is part of our life. Because sometimes we're in the afterlife, sometimes in the hereafter.

- Will I be like him?

- You can feel what your physical body will be like. You know what you deserve better than I do, replied Nenvis calmly. - But we have many ways of redeeming our mistakes, and the best way is by doing good. If Nenê hadn't been so upset when he was disincarnated, he might have chosen another way to redeem his imprudence. Nothing in spirituality is a general rule; people can have disabilities by choice, by trial... There are many reasons.

- I don't think my reincarnation will be easy at all.

Realizing that this spirit was concerned about this fact, Nenvis insisted on this subject, leaving him pensive. Afterwards, the group leader took him to visit several homes, where the ex-employee noticed the difference in the ways of living.

- Here - Nenvis showed - there are reincarnated spirits who are learning to be useful. These others will have to experience greater pain as a learning experience, and if they don't redeem their mistakes through love and doing good, pain will come to try to teach them.

The ex-employee paid close attention. Taking advantage of the fact that he was less rancorous, the group leader asked:

- Where and how are the two spirits you murdered?

- How? - he was startled.

- Didn't you murder two people? Didn't you put an end to their physical existence? Did they want to die?

- No! I don't think they wanted to die. I don't know about them. Why did I forget about these two men? I didn't think about them. I only thought that I had been murdered.

- That happens, replied Nenvis. - We have to pay attention to our attitudes because they belong to us.

- They didn't want revenge! Have they forgiven me?

- They certainly forgave you and went off to look after themselves. If you change the direction of your life, you may learn about these two spirits in the future and perhaps one day ask for forgiveness.

- I should have remembered them and followed their example. It would certainly have been much better for me, I would have been happier, said the ex-employee, regretting it.

- You can change.

He asked to go to a shelter, said he had forgiven them, that he wanted to ask for forgiveness and improve himself. Nenvis took him to a help center on the threshold. He soon went from shelter worker to helper. He enjoyed working and became a good helper. With his companions, he went all over the threshold around the post, helping suffering spirits. Without the presence of his former obsessors, Nenê felt more at ease. The team continued to visit him.

One day he was moaning and they realized he had a toothache. His sister was able to receive Maria's intuition and took him to the dentist, who decided to extract all his teeth. Nenê disincarnated five years after they saw him for the first time. His change of plane was smooth, he was rescued and taken to a colony. He didn't stay long on the spiritual plane and was reincarnated, this time in a healthy body.

They always had a lot to do. As well as taking care of requests, and many of them were laborious, the team helped the helpers at the small aid station in the cemetery and the hospital. They also used the time to study.

Noeli loved what she did.

# Chapter 15

# *WORK DONE*

The team was united by a sincere friendship, because everyone had the same goal: to do good. Noeli took the opportunity to learn; she was really interested and knowledge was consolidated. She got to know other teams who, like theirs, attended to requests. In the town church, João and four disincarnates tried to help in the name of our Lady, Jesus, Saint Anthony and other saints.

- João, explained Nenvis, is very dedicated and has been working for fifty years answering requests made to the mother of Jesus.

Noeli enjoyed meeting him. Talking to him was like receiving lessons.

- When he was incarnate, said João, he was devoted to our Lady. When I was discarnate, I wanted to know how the mother of Jesus assisted so many people. I met teams working in her name. I studied and prepared myself to be part of a group of workers who fulfill requests made to Mary of Nazareth. I really love what I do. Over the years, the team has changed all the time. Some come, others go. The simplest cases, we attend to ourselves; the more difficult ones, a counselor comes from the colony to help us. Unfortunately, we can't deal with every request. Some are like a child who asks to play with a sharp knife and, if they receive it, they could get hurt.

- I know this, said Noeli. - Yesterday a woman asked me to make her husband's mistress sick, to make her get cancer.

- Not even half an hour ago, we received a request to punish, to bring justice to a murderer. If they understood the law of action and reaction, they would understand that this murderer must be repaid. What is certain is that they should pray for the disincarnate who was the victim and ask our Lady to help them forgive and love. All those who pray are helped - João continued to explain - sometimes we can't or don't manage to fulfill what they ask for, but we try to guide them, giving them benevolent energies.

- This woman, said Noeli, who asked for her husband's mistress to fall ill, we tried to calm her down, we talked to her tonight and asked her to be patient, not to wish harm on anyone and to take care of her health. This morning, we managed to intuit a friend of hers, who came to see us and gave her good advice. We will visit her more often and urge her to pray and think good thoughts.

João and the team were also working at the aid station. Nenvis took Noeli to the department of the colony where they received requests. The place is spacious, with several desks and a large table in the center. At the entrance, a receptionist writes down the requests of the discarnate.

- Do the residents of the colony also ask for graces? - asked Noeli in amazement.

- Yes, replied Nenvis, not only from the colony, but also from the aid workers who come here seeking help. The department receives requests from incarnate people as well as those who live on the spiritual plane and are wandering and those who are suffering. The spirits who come here usually ask for family members, friends who are still on the physical plane or for discarnate loved ones who are wandering or suffering on the threshold. And, as with all petitions, they are analyzed and answered according to need.

- Is it valid to pray for someone else?

- We can pray for help for other people. Each case is different. For example, a mother asking for help for her little boy who doesn't yet know how to pray. We receive many requests from sick people who can't pray either. Many requests are granted in these cases. However, I would remind you again that when we find receptivity, it is easier for the person to receive. See that lady? - Nenvis showed a woman who was sitting in the waiting room. - She comes here a lot and asks for her son who is on the threshold. But he lives in the threshold zone and, at the moment, he says he likes it there and doesn't want another life. The mother is usually persistent, and the department's counselor told me that he will soon take her to her son so that she can talk to him. That's what the department staff can do for this lady.

- There are so many requests! - said Noeli in amazement.

Both on the table and on the desks, there were piles of requests.

- Everything is very organized here, said Nenvis. Noeli, seeing the work of several helpers, understood that those who pray with faith really do become receptive to their requests. Often, they don't receive what they ask for, but the answer to their prayer is the help they need at the moment. Many receive what they asked for. The department is staffed by many disincarnates; some petitions are answered by themselves; and others are taken to teams working close to the petitioner. Most of the requests made in Brazil are for Our Lady, and there are many teams of helpers who attend in her name. A veritable legion of workers who learn a lot through these tasks.

- Does the mother of Jesus, Mary, attend to any requests? - Noeli wanted to know.

- Mary is an active spirit, a tireless worker, a loving mother, she is always visiting the teams, encouraging them and thanking them for attending on her behalf. I think that, on some occasions, she does. These are real graces.

Noeli also learned that, normally, in these departments, there is always a more experienced team that joins others to resolve more complex issues. She really enjoyed getting to know these departments.

Violeta was always with her daughter, she still lived in the colony, worked in the hospital and studied hard. It was a joy when she visited the team.

João Luiz also visited them.

- Godmother, he said, I've learned to love Gracia as a sister, as I wanted to. She loves her husband and now they're well. I visit her and help her when I can. I'm now part of a team that helps people in rural areas. I'm really enjoying this work. I want to ask to be reincarnated with them, to be the son of a girl who will soon become a girl and, of course, get married. My counselor told me that it could work.

João Luiz, as always, was enthusiastic: he was active and used his free time to study and devote himself to agronomy. He was taken care of: years later, he was reincarnated into his chosen family. Noeli visited him; he was a beautiful, healthy boy.

She knew about his friends, visited them whenever possible and talked a lot with the aid workers. Father Ambrózio used to see them. He asked not to be called "priest" anymore.

- "Father", "priest"... I was when I was incarnate. Here I am just Ambrózio, the apprentice.

Ambrózio dedicated himself to helping, he stayed in the colony, studied and worked in the hospital.

After Ambrózio disincarnated, the town was without a priest for three months. Then an elderly priest arrived to stay on temporarily, but he ended up staying for three years and four months. This priest carried out his duties as a priest, but without getting involved in the community's problems. Finding it difficult to fulfill his duties, he asked to return to the convent. Once again, the town was left without a priest for eight months. The priest from the neighboring metropolis came to celebrate Mass on Sundays. A young priest was appointed to take Ambrózio's place. He worked hard to organize everything and put everything in order.

But, as there are always "buts", he paid attention to the graces that his parishioners received from the Little Saint. He wanted to know who she was. Several women told him about Noeli's life, the graces that many people had received and asked to have her sanctified.

- It would be very good for us and for the town to have a saint, enthused a woman.

The priest didn't like what he heard or the enthusiasm of his parishioners.

- This woman, the priest concluded, cannot be a saint.

She wasn't Catholic.

- Yes, she was - said the other woman - she was baptized, Father Ambrózio blessed her body when she died.

- She didn't go to church, she didn't go to mass, she didn't go to confession or take communion. She can't be a saint!

Thinking it was absurd for his parishioners to make a pilgrimage to the cemetery at Noeli's grave, asking for graces, the priest first advised:

- The place for prayers is in the church, which is the house of God. Requests and prayers should be made to God, to Jesus, to the Virgin Mary and to the saints.

He talked a lot with the people, especially the women, and ended up forbidding it.

- This is sacrilege! It's a sin! Anyone who goes to this woman's tomb should go to confession, because they have sinned.

The wig with Noeli's hair, after Mariana healed, was passed on to several people who, even though they had hair, used it to heal from some illness.

There was even a waiting list. So, they started cutting their hair and each person got a strand. Many people healed or felt better as a result of the fluids received from the team. The priest ended up taking the wig, which was ugly because it had been cut so many times, and put it in the fire; also threatening that it was a sin, he took several strands of hair and burned them.

Some people began to sneak to the tomb, and the flowers and requests dwindled. One afternoon, Nenvis and Noeli overheard two women talking in front of the tomb.

- I've come to pay my promise. Although the priest told me that I didn't have to pay anything because I hadn't received any grace from Little Saint. I was in doubt and, just in case, I thought it best to come and pay. A promise is a debt! I'm not going to ask Little Saint for anything more.

- Don't call her that anymore, advised the other woman

- the priest doesn't want to; he says Sofia isn't a saint. And if we insist, we'll be excommunicated.

- What does that even mean?

- I looked it up in the dictionary and found out that it's a penalty that excludes one from the sacraments and prayers of the church and from the enjoyment of some spiritual goods. The excommunicated person is cursed, separated from the church forever. And, as the priest says, he will go to hell.

- Does the church have such power? - asked the promise payer.

- I don't know, but I'm afraid. I don't want to go to hell because of that.

The two of them immediately left the tomb; Noeli, curious, asked her advisor:

- Have you ever seen an excommunicate? Do you know what happens to them?

- I was excommunicated once. In 1649, when I was reincarnated in Spain, I was a priest; because I didn't agree with the attitudes of my superiors and because I drew attention to them, I was excommunicated, arrested and poisoned. It didn't make any difference to me, I disincarnated with good feelings, I asked God for forgiveness and I did, I was helped and I was fine on the spiritual plane. However, a cellmate, also a priest, received the same sentence as me for having acted wrongly by getting involved with a girl from an influential family. We died together from the same poison. He felt excommunicated and wandered around suffering for years. Whether or not you feel this curse depends on your feelings; for the good, it won't make any difference, and for the reckless, it's his attitudes that will make you suffer.

The priest really didn't want them to pray to the Blessed Virgin. João, the church staff leader, was worried about the priest; he wouldn't accept them even when his spirit was away from his sleeping body. This priest didn't accept opinions contrary to his own, he was very radical.

- Everything has a cycle, concluded Nenvis, our work in this community is coming to an end. This was foreseen. The time has come to reincarnate.

Nenvis, Maria, Carlos and Clara planned to return to the physical plane. They started going to the Colony to study, they wanted to prepare themselves well to return to dense matter. Nenvis would return to the physical plane first and, two years or so later, Carlos, who would become his brother. Maria would be the daughter of a couple close to Nenvis' parents. Clara would be reincarnated in the same city. The group's advisor and Maria planned to get married and have Violeta and Noeli as their daughters. Clara and Carlos also planned to be together.

- Is everyone planning their reincarnation? - Noeli wanted to know.

- Unfortunately, not, replied Nenvis. - When the inhabitants of Earth evolve more, this will happen, as it does on planets whose inhabitants are more evolved.

Many plans are made, but we can't be sure that they will happen like this. Maria and I, for example, are kindred spirits, we are planning to reincarnate and unite, but this may or may not happen. We may not meet for various reasons, such as a family move, or we may meet and our union doesn't work out, or one of us may be interested in someone else?

- And then what? Whose daughter will I be? - Noeli asked.

- You'll have to choose to be my daughter or Maria's or even someone else's. What I want you to understand is that we can plan, but plans don't always come true because we have free will. In my last incarnation, I planned to be the son of a friend, in an attempt to help him as a loving son. He committed suicide when he was eighteen.

- What happened to your plans? - Noeli was curious.

- I helped him all I could, replied Nenvis. - But the suicidal person has to pay for his mistake. We couldn't be together anymore. I reincarnated into another family and expanded my circle of friends. But to answer your previous question, not everyone today can plan their incarnation. Only spirits who have dedicated themselves to doing good, who have studied and consolidated what they have learned in their work by being useful, can plan in more detail. I have seen rebellious disincarnates who, feeling they have to return to the physical plane, stay close to similar incarnates and reincarnate at the first opportunity. We then see children and teenagers committing evil deeds. Some disincarnates are so disturbed that workers in the Reincarnation Department plan their return to matter. Most only make plans without much foundation or conviction. Example: a spirit has been helped, but has not been interested in studying or being useful, and has spent years carrying on as he did in incarnate life, being served. It makes plans: "I'll be reincarnated in this family whose father is my friend or whose mother was once my sister. I'm going to study medicine and dedicate myself to caring for the sick." In incarnate, they often find it difficult to study, so they go and do something else, or, if they study medicine, they only look at the financial side. There are many temptations that lead many people not to do what they had planned. Another example is those who want to have mediumship in order to work for good: while incarnate, they don't want it and don't do anything with it. These are usually superfluous plans, unlike those who really wish it, plan it, study it and put it into practice with a firm will. However, these plans cannot be seen as fatal events. A friend of mine planned to be a heart patient as soon as he became an adult, reincarnated and, in his youth, dedicated himself to humanitarian work. Praying a lot and receiving blessings of thanks, he didn't fall ill. Another person he knew would be healthy, but he started to get drunk and disincarnated ten years ahead of schedule, very sick. In this way, we change what was planned for better or for worse.

- I noticed that you, Carlos, Clara and Grandma Maria are often apprehensive about being reincarnated. Why is that? - Noeli asked.

- We don't have a guilty conscience, don't feel remorse or have wrongdoings to make up for. Just so you understand, we don't have negative karma. However, we do have tests to overcome, and there are many. A student who has studied and thinks he knows the whole subject is still apprehensive before the exam. We're in this situation: we know the theory, but what about the practice? Will we do what we planned to do to the best of our ability? Will we be able to overcome the difficulties that will arise? The physical plane offers many illusions and temptations.

- As I understand it, you'd like to live forever on the spiritual plane, wouldn't you?

- That's not it - Nenvis smiled - we know that we have to be tested by ourselves periodically. We are spirits who are still in the process of earthly reincarnations, sometimes there, sometimes here.

- Yesterday, said Noeli, at the aid station, Maria Ines was euphoric because she was about to be reincarnated soon. She told me that she wasn't used to the spiritual plane and wanted to live on the physical plane. I was amazed.

- Most inhabitants of the earth enjoy life in the flesh, the pleasures that the body offers. There are many spirits who want to reincarnate, and the reasons are diverse. There are those who want to prove to themselves that they have learned their lesson, just like us, and most of them are worried and apprehensive when faced with trials. Others, feeling remorse, whose pain is really deep, want the blessing of oblivion and to redeem their mistakes, often suffering what they made the other suffer. Some want the physical envelope in order to be in contact with their enemies or loved ones, and others think of enjoying pleasures or simply enjoy life in the flesh.

Noeli wondered.

- Of course, like Noelli, before suffering as a lesson, I was selfish and, of course, if I could choose, I would want to be beautiful and rich. Blessed is the pain that teaches. I hope to learn from now on only through love.

Faced with the priest's threats, the requests diminished. Nevis reincarnated; so, did Maria, Carlos and Clara. Only Noeli and Leocácio remained and, when they needed help, rescuers from the aid station helped them.

Noeli began to think about her reincarnation. She was afraid of making mistakes again. She would have beauty of a normal standard and would be able to study. She didn't plan what she would study. She learned that most people on the spiritual plane didn't choose what they would study or work in. He wanted to have a profession that would be useful and that, as well as providing for him, would help people. Like Carlos, Clara, Nenvis and Maria, she didn't have someone in mind, a kindred spirit, to join with. He learned that most spirits didn't plan this commitment. There were few who committed to being together. She wanted to find someone to love and be loved by, get married and have children, she wanted to be a mother. Her plans were few: she wanted to be helped when she disincarnated, but to achieve this wish, she would have to earn it.

She dedicated more time to her studies, she visited the colony frequently, wanted to learn more and started working a few hours in the library. As time went by, there were many times when Noeli felt afraid of returning to the physical plane, of proving to herself that she wanted to be useful by doing something good.

- Will I be able to? Will I be useful? I don't want to do anything bad.

One afternoon, deep in thought, she opened The Gospel according to Spiritism and read: "Understand the great role of humanity, understand that when a body is generated, the soul that reincarnates in it comes from space to progress. Perform your duties and put all your love into bringing that soul closer to God: this is the mission entrusted to you and you will receive the reward if you fulfill it faithfully."[12]

- I hope that I will be received like this - Noeli wished fervently - that I will be educated and given good religious guidance. My God! I'm thinking about myself, about what I want to receive. I must meditate on this text in order to receive

---

[12] N.A.E.: Chapter 14, "Honor your father and mother", "The ingratitude of children and the bonds of family" to be served. Thank you, God, for the opportunity of reincarnation.

my children and educate them. Think about giving, serving, because only in this way will I move towards progress.

Years later, with her future parents in their teens and dating, Noeli left her work with the incarnate for good and went to the colony to study and prepare for reincarnation. Grateful and feeling at peace, she took one last look at the grave, which had only three flowers on it, and smiled. She would never go there again; if she had asked, the team of helpers at the aid station and Leocácio would have responded.

- It's a good thing I've never been there! - she exclaimed. - I say goodbye gratefully, I've listened and learned a lot here.

She left hopeful and happy.

THE END

www.ingramcontent.com/pod-product-compliance
Lightning Source LLC
LaVergne TN
LVHW041759060526
838201LV00046B/1058